Susan M. Ewing

77
Things to Know
Before Getting a Cat

The Essential Guide to
Preparing Your Family and Home
for a Feline Companion

77 Things to Know Before Getting a Cat

CompanionHouse Books™ is an imprint of Fox Chapel Publishers International Ltd.

Project Team
Vice President–Content: Christopher Reggio
Editor: Amy Deputato
Copy Editor: Laura Taylor
Design: Llara Pazdan
Index: Elizabeth Walker

ISBN 978-1-62008-291-1

Library of Congress Cataloging-in-Publication Data

Names: Ewing, Susan M., author.
Title: 77 things to know before getting a cat : the essential guide to
    preparing your family and home for a feline companion / by Susan Ewing.
Other titles: Seventy seven things to know before getting a cat
Description: Mount Joy, PA : CompanionHouse Books, an imprint of Fox Chapel
    Publishers International Ltd, [2018] | Includes index.
Identifiers: LCCN 2018032320 (print) | LCCN 2018034689 (ebook) | ISBN
    9781620082928 (ebook) | ISBN 9781620082911 (softcover)
Subjects: LCSH: Cats. | Cat adoption.
Classification: LCC SF447 (ebook) | LCC SF447 .E95 2018 (print) | DDC
    636.8/0887--dc23
LC record available at https://lccn.loc.gov/2018032320

This book has been published with the intent to provide accurate and authoritative information in regard to the subject matter within. While every precaution has been taken in the preparation of this book, the author and publisher expressly disclaim any responsibility for any errors, omissions, or adverse effects arising from the use or application of the information contained herein. The techniques and suggestions are used at the reader's discretion and are not to be considered a substitute for veterinary care. If you suspect a medical problem, consult your veterinarian.

Fox Chapel Publishing
903 Square Street
Mount Joy, PA 17552

Fox Chapel Publishers International Ltd.
7 Danefield Road, Selsey (Chichester)
West Sussex PO20 9DA, U.K.

www.facebook.com/companionhousebooks

We are always looking for talented authors. To submit an idea, please send a brief inquiry to acquisitions@foxchapelpublishing.com.

Printed and bound in China
20 19 18 17   2 4 6 8 10 9 7 5 3 1

Contents

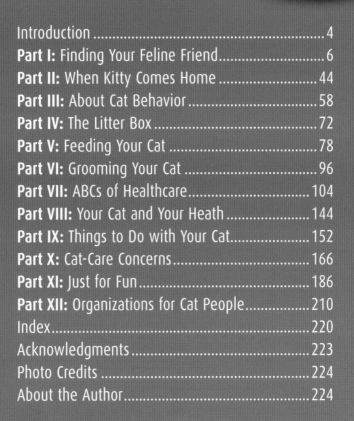

Introduction
First Things First...

This is not a training manual, nor is it a book on breeding and raising kittens, and it is definitely not a veterinary handbook. It is a book with information that can make owning your first cat easier.

Do you really need to know seventy-seven things before getting a cat? No. You definitely need to know a few things, though, and then there are some other things that will make life with your cat more enjoyable. Some of the things in this book are helpful, while others are simply interesting or just for fun.

First-time cat owners will find essential information on a variety of topics, such as recommended vaccinations and the pros and cons of different types of food. There's a list of poisonous plants and ideas on how to teach your cat to use a scratching post.

Then there's information you might want to know just because your cat fascinates you. You might want to know about the origin of cats or read about some superstitions surrounding cats. Can you own a certain cat breed without knowing that its official colors are lavender and cream? Sure! But doesn't lavender and cream sound more elegant than light gray and pale orange?

Maybe the title of this book should be *Several Things to Know before Getting a Cat,* and *Several More Things That Are Just Fun to Know.* You can never know enough about this fascinating species.

A few additional notes: People tend to call dogs "he" and cats "she," but I refer to cats as "he" unless I'm talking about a specific cat. That's because, in general, male cats are more affectionate, and a male may make a better first cat for someone than a female would. I refer to all breeders as "she" because women seem to be in the majority in that field. The same goes for veterinarians. Women may not be in the majority in the field of veterinary medicine, but I've known some terrific women veterinarians, so I've chosen to refer to veterinarians using "she."

Also, sometimes I talk about situations involving multiple cats. Yes, this book is for first-time cat owners, but, for many people, one cat is like one potato chip. You want another, and another after that. Whether you stop at one or add a few more, this book will give you a head start on living with a happy, healthy cat.

PART I

Finding Your Feline Friend

Do You Really Want a Cat? 1

Before you get a cat, think about why you want one. Cats are not little dogs, nor are they small people in fur coats. Maybe you have problems with mice and think that a cat is the answer. Certainly, cats are known to hunt mice, but some cats are more predatory than others. You may get one like Garfield, the cartoon cat, who just lazily watches mice run by. Get a cat only if you want to enjoy the cat himself, not just because he may have hunting potential.

In contrast, maybe you're horrified at the thought of your pet hunting rodents. Whether you plan to keep your cat always indoors (and there are many good reasons to do so) or he is allowed outdoors, he will most likely present you with a tiny corpse from time to time. Cats are carnivores and hunters. If the thought of a dead mouse or songbird upsets you, a cat may not be your ideal pet.

Maybe you've fallen in love with the idea of a kitten from all of the photos and videos you've seen online. Kittens are irresistible, but they need care, and they don't stay kittens forever. They grow into cats who may or may not be as adorable.

Children may be the number-one reason that people get cats. Most children love the idea of having a pet, and parents may think that cats are less work than dogs. While most cats *are* less work than most dogs, that doesn't mean there's

no effort involved. Don't get a cat if you are not willing to be his primary caretaker. Even if your child promises to take care of the new addition, the ultimate responsibility is yours.

Also, while a cat and your kids can make a great combination, not every cat will appreciate the attentions of children. Children need to be taught to respect the cat and his claws. If your children are very young, it might be better to wait a bit before introducing a cat—or any pet—into the family.

If you don't want cat hair on your furniture, don't get a cat. Some cats don't shed, and some shed more than others, but if you have a cat, you will likely have cat hair around your home. And don't forget the possibility of hairballs. There's nothing quite like getting up in the middle of the night

Are you ready to share your lap with a feline friend?

and feeling a hairball squish between your naked toes.

If you think a cat would provide a touch of elegance to your decor, buy an antique vase instead. What happens if you change your decor? Do you get rid of the cat? Besides, a cat may have the opposite effect if he decides to sharpen his claws on your love seat or shred your drapes. There are ways to prevent that type of destructive behavior, but if you're very concerned with interior decorating, you might not appreciate scratching posts or a cat tree in your living room. And as for that antique vase, cats have been known to push things off shelves. If you have many breakable treasures, you may not want a cat.

Consider the expense of owning a cat. You'll want to spay or neuter as well as keep your feline up to date on all recommended vaccinations.

You'll need monthly heartworm-preventive medication and protection from fleas and ticks in addition to regular veterinary checkups. An illness or injury might require additional trips to the vet's office. Consider grooming: will you cut your cat's claws yourself or take him to a groomer? If you're on a fixed income or will begrudge the money you spend on your cat's care, food, and accessories, rethink the idea of a cat.

If you are a vegetarian or a vegan, that's fine; however, if you want your pet also to be vegetarian or vegan, do not get a cat. Cats need meat. There is no long-term substitute that will work to keep a cat in good condition. If you are not prepared to feed meat to your cat, don't get a cat.

The bottom line is that a cat is a living being that needs care and attention. He needs good food, clean water, shelter, and veterinary care. Also, just because a cat is typically easier to care for than some other types of pets doesn't mean that you can ignore your cat.

No matter how much your child loves the cat, she cannot be his primary caretaker.

Cats may not be as overtly affectionate as dogs, but they do bond with their people, and they do enjoy the company of their families. Isolating or neglecting a cat is cruel.

There's a wonderful children's book by Margaret Mahy called *The Three-Legged Cat*. In the story, a woman has a three-legged cat, but she isn't always happy with him because he sheds and eats a lot. The woman has a brother who wanders the world, but the brother has decided to retire from travel because his old fur hat doesn't keep his head as warm as it used to. After a visit with his sister, the man mistakenly puts the cat on his head, leaving his old hat behind. The woman is delighted. She can hold the hat on her lap and stroke it, but it doesn't shed and it never eats.

Maybe you're like that woman. If you just want something warm in your lap that you can pet, a stuffed animal can do the job. There are even toy cats that move and purr. These alternatives are cuddly and entertaining, with never a litter box to clean or a tin of cat food to open.

2 Origin of the Cat

All carnivores, including felines and canines, evolved from a common ancestor, the miacoids, which existed from 66 to 33 million years ago. The first true feline didn't make an appearance until about 30 million years ago. According to an article on *MessyBeast.com* titled "Prehistoric Cats and Prehistoric Cat-Like Creatures" by Sarah Hartwell, this was Proailurus, a long-bodied, short-legged animal. Ten million years later, Pseudaelurus arrived on the scene, and it is generally believed that Pseudaelurus is the ancestor of all modern-day cats.

The genus Felis arrived about 12 million years ago and gave rise to many kinds of small cats, known as "purring cats," for the obvious reason that they purr. Three million years ago, the "roaring cats" of the genus *Panthera* appeared. Modern-day "roaring cats" are generally big cats, like lions and tigers. The cheetah, however, is a big cat who purrs. Because of their throat structure, cats who purr do not roar, and cats who roar are unable to purr.

Prehistoric cats roamed throughout Asia, Europe, and North and South America, but many types became extinct. Genetic evidence indicates that all domestic cats are descended from the African wildcat (*Felis silvestris lybica*). These cats, weighing between 6–14 pounds (2.7 and 6.4 kg), still exist throughout Africa and the Middle East in a variety of habitats. They look similar to today's tabby cat but with a reddish tinge to the ears, the abdomen, and the backs of the hind legs.

Most of today's big cats are classified as "roaring cats."

Domesticated cats helped farmers with rodent control.

Domestication began between 10 and 12 thousand years ago in the Fertile Crescent as humans started to settle rather than lead nomadic lives. Instead of depending on wild sources of food, people began growing, harvesting, and storing grains. These stores of food drew rodents, and the rodents drew the cats, who were happy to find a concentrated food source that required less energy to catch than prey in the wild.

The farmers were more than happy to have the cats around to help protect their grain. Because humans offered no threat to the cats, the cats gradually moved closer and closer to human settlements, taking up residence near the grain stores and eventually becoming domesticated.

Through the years, what started out as a tabby wild cat has evolved, with man's help, into a species that ranges in size from 4 to more than 20 pounds (1.8–9.1 kg), has a seemingly endless number of colors and color combination, and has a variety of coat types or no coat at all. Cats are still appreciated for their rodent-killing skills but they are mainly loved for their grace, beauty, and companion-pet qualities that offer gentle affection as well as entertainment.

Today's African wildcat, *Felis silvestris lybica.*

3 Indoors or Outdoors?

Cats are hunters by nature, and they love roaming the great outdoors. The problem is that the great outdoors doesn't always love your cat. An outdoor cat runs the risk of being hit by a car; being chased, hurt, or killed by a dog; and ingesting pesticides, rodent poison, or other harmful substances. There's also the risk of a fight with another cat, which can lead to serious bite and scratch wounds or catching a disease. Your cat can pick up external parasites, such as fleas and ticks, and internal parasites (various types of worms) from another cat. Because cats like to hunt at night, they're more likely to encounter wild animals that may have rabies or that may cause deadly injuries to your cat. Humans can pose a threat as well. If your cat is using your neighbor's garden for a toilet, the neighbor may retaliate in some way.

Whether you allow your cat outdoors will depend on where you live, and many cats enjoy a combination of indoor and outdoor living, but owners must keep the risks in mind. If you choose to let your cat roam outdoors, be sure to use a flea and tick preventive and keep your cat up to date on all vaccinations. *Never* let a declawed cat go outdoors. He will be totally defenseless.

If you've decided that your cat will be an indoors-only cat, you need to do more than just supply cat food and a litter box. Cats need attention, exercise, and something to do. If you've got a screened-in porch or a sunroom, you can turn it into your cat's play area. Make a small obstacle course for your cat with boxes and boards to create tunnels, jumps, and walkways. Use a wand toy to entice your cat to play. Hide tasty treats around the home; your cat will enjoy the hunt, and trying to find those treats will give your cat some exercise. You could even hide your cat's food bowl in a different place each day, giving the cat something to hunt.

Another great way to encourage your cat to use his mind is by giving him food puzzles. A food puzzle is a type of toy that dispenses bits of food as your cat turns and twists it.

There are some risks involved with allowing your cat to roam outdoors.

A snuffle mat is another way to keep your cat busy. This is a soft mat with many little pockets and folds for hiding dry food or treats.

Many people build "catios" for their cats; a catio is an outside screened room that may contain a small tree or some shrubs, giving a cat a place to enjoy fresh air without being in any danger. You could install a cat tunnel to give your cat protected access to the outdoors. A cat tunnel attaches at one end to a pet door and is closed at the other end. It is made of see-through mesh so that your cat can see what's going on around him and get some fresh air. If you opt for something like this, lock the pet door when you're not at home because a determined animal, including the cat, can tear though the mesh. You don't want your cat getting out, or another animal getting in.

Another option for safe outdoor time is cat fencing. This type of fencing attaches to existing fencing and curves inward so that a climbing cat can't go up and over. You can also get a cat harness and take your cat for on-leash walks. Many cats enjoy strolls around the neighborhood. Start when your cat is young so that he's used to the harness and the leash. Never use a collar—always use a harness, which is more secure.

If you use a leash, never tie your cat out and leave him unattended. He can easily get tangled and seriously injure himself—plus, being tied to a specific spot leaves him vulnerable to attack by other animals.

Toys give indoor cats physical and mental activity.

For indoor play, remember that cats enjoy visual stimulation. Some cats will watch television and may enjoy nature programs. You can show your cats videos of birds and small animals that may attract his attention. If you'd enjoy an aquarium, so will your cat—just make sure that the tank has a secure lid so that your cat can't help himself to fishy snacks. A bird feeder outside a window is something else your cat will enjoy.

ANOTHER PET

If you decide to get another cat, or you already have a dog, this will hopefully give your cat a playmate, or at least someone to take a nap with.

You have multiple factors to consider when deciding on what type of cat you want. Cats don't have the size range that you find in dogs. Instead of weighing between 2 and 200 pounds, most cats fall between 4 and 20 pounds (1.8–9.1 kg). Whether you prefer a smaller, more delicate feline, or you have your heart set on a heftier animal, there's not going to be much difference in how much space either cat needs for comfort.

The Turkish Van's abundant coat sheds minimally.

Maybe you're concerned about hair. If a cat has hair, he will shed, but some cats shed less than others. Or you might select a hairless breed, such as the Sphynx or the Devon Rex. The Cornish Rex has a very light, curly coat with minimal shedding, and Russian Blues, LaPerms, Siamese, Tonkinese, and Bengals also shed minimally. According to CatTime (*www.cattime.com*), even the longhaired Turkish Van is a light shedder, so, if you want a cat with a longer coat but are worried about shedding, the Turkish Van might be a good choice.

If you do choose a hairless or sparsely coated breed, remember that your cat will need protection from the cold, which may mean a sweater or coat if you live where there are cold winters. All cats must have shelter, but hairless breeds will do best living entirely indoors.

You shouldn't base your choice solely on whether or not the cat sheds, though. Consider the personality of the breed and the individual cat. Bengals, for instance, are high-energy cats that need exercise. Ragdolls are at the other extreme—perfectly happy to lie quietly and be admired. If you're selecting a pedigreed cat, do some research about what it's like to live with a particular breed. In the larger scheme of things, I'd rather have a cat whose personality was a good fit even if it meant more hair on the furniture, but that's something you need to decide before you get a cat.

The Sphynx is a hairless cat breed.

The striking Siamese is a popular breed.

Another consideration is whether to get a male or female. There will be exceptions, but cat owners generally agree that males are more affectionate than females. Affection doesn't matter if a cat lives in a barn as a mouser, but most people who have pet cats prefer their cats to show some affection.

In their book, *Your Ideal Cat: Insights into Breed and Gender Differences in Cat Behavior*, authors Benjamin L. Hart, DVM, PhD, and Lynette A. Hart, PhD, rank some cat breeds according to how affectionate they are. The Ragdoll scored the highest, followed by the domestic shorthair, Burmese, and Maine Coon. Least likely to show affection were the Bengal, Manx, and Abyssinian. Still, many owners of cat breeds that aren't known for showing affection will argue that their cats are affectionate. Members of the Cat Writers' Association to whom I spoke were all in agreement that a cat's affectionate and outgoing temperament is the result of both genetics and living

environment. It partially depends on how much, and what kind of, affection you expect from your cat.

Teresa Keiger, editor of *Cat Talk* magazine, notes that some breeds are more gregarious than others, and some are more cautious around strangers. "Russian Blues are [more cautious]. They also bond closely with their owners . . . and are a classic example of what breeding to improve temperament can achieve. Breeding for temperament changed their demeanor."

Keiger discusses another factor that influences an individual cat's personality. "The usual 'pecking order' is whole females, whole males, spays, neuters. Genetics plays a huge role in temperament, and breeders take that into consideration in their breeding programs. I would not be surprised to learn that sensory input played a role in temperament." She also says, "Another factor is exposure to various and frequent stimuli from an early age. Kittens exposed to a higher level of noise and activity generally seem to be less shy than ones raised in a quiet environment. So, it's nature and nurture."

While Bev Caldwell, retired feline health and behavior writer and longtime

Russian Blue kitten.

owner of pedigreed cats, agrees that males are generally more affectionate, she adds that it also depends on the individual cat and probably whether the owner has had the cat from kittenhood or has adopted an adult cat. Sometimes adult shelter cats may come with bad habits or may have temperaments shaped by previous mistreatment, such as being removed from their mothers too early or being neglected by former owners.

Being regarded as more affectionate gives males an edge over females, but, on the negative side, males are much more likely than females to spray their urine. It's a way of marking their territory. Neutering helps, but may not totally extinguish, spraying behavior.

Regardless of breed and sex, all cats will have their good and bad points. It's a good idea to research breeds and to consider what traits you can and can't live with. In the end, though, you may have decided on a shorthaired male Siamese only to be captivated by a female domestic longhair. Do your homework—but it's also OK to listen to your heart.

AFFECTION MATTERS

Take into account both the breed and the sex, but don't ignore the power of affection and attention as it relates to your cat's temperament.

How affectionate a cat is varies by breed and individual.

5 Kitty Colors

Colors in cats are almost as mysterious as the cat itself. To make things even more interesting, different breeds have different names for the same colors. Add different patterns into the mix, and you have an almost infinite variety.

The cat's basic colors are black, red, and brown. Red may be called "flame," and black is described as "ebony" in some breed standards. From the basics, you get into dilute shades and all of their hues. Blue is a dilute color of black. Indigo is a dark blue or gray, and lavender and lilac are the same: a soft pinkish-gray.

Abyssinian cats display a ticked tabby pattern.

A silver cat in a tabby pattern.

Patterns include solid, tabby, pointed, piebald, and van, but it's not that simple. For instance, in the van pattern, the cat is white with a colored tail, color over the ears and top of the head, and possibly a spot of color on the back. The colored fur can be a solid color or in a tabby pattern.

There are four tabby patterns: mackerel, classic, spotted, and ticked, all of which have a mark on the forehead resembling an "M." The mackerel tabby is the most common, with narrow stripes of a darker color on a slightly lighter background and dark bands on the legs and tail. The classic tabby has more of a bull's-eye pattern on the sides and a dark center stripe along the spine as well as the dark bands on the legs and tail.

A ticked tabby pattern lacks the stripes of the mackerel and classic and has hairs with distinct bands of color on them. These agouti hairs give a textured look of light and dark to the coat. The Abyssinian is an example of a ticked tabby.

In the spotted tabby pattern, the stripes are broken up to look like spots. The Bengal, Ocicat, and Egyptian Mau are examples of this kind of pattern.

Pointed, or colorpoint, cats include the Siamese, Burmese, Himalayan, and Ragdoll. True colorpoint cats always have blue eyes. According to the Cat Fanciers Association, Siamese cats may have seal (almost black), chocolate (warm brown), blue (slate blue), and lilac (pinkish-gray); the International Cat Association additionally recognizes red, cream, and tabby points.

In all colorpoint cats, the color is the result of a gene that inhibits pigment. This gene is affected by temperature; the dark color comes out on the cooler body areas, like the tail, face, and legs. As a pointed cat ages, the skin temperature cools and the body darkens.

Piebald cats have two or more distinct colors, generally on a white background. Tortoiseshell cats, or "torties," are cats whose fur combines two colors other than white, usually black and red or the dilute variations of these colors. Our neighbor's beautiful tortie would be described as lavender/lilac and cream.

If the tabby pattern is also in evidence, the cat is called a "torbie."

Colors vary according to registry and can be put together into many combinations. For example, the American Cat Fanciers Association lists thirty-nine possible color combinations plus "and white" and "van-colored" for the American Shorthair, which includes fifteen tabby variations, such as brown, blue, cameo, golden, and silver. Besides the standard black, blue, red and cream, there's also chinchilla, cameo, blue smoke, black smoke, and blue cream smoke.

The classic tortoiseshell colors are black and red.

A green-eyed beauty.

Other cats may be cinnamon, or amber, or fawn. And these are just coat colors. Cats' eyes may be blue, copper, green, gold, or brown, or a cat may have eyes of two different colors. This can occur in any breed, but is frequently seen in the Turkish Angora, Turkish Van, and Japanese Bobtail.

If you want to study all of the various permutations of color in cats, the Messy Beast's color charts (*www.messybeast.com/colour-charts.htm*) are a great place to start. If you're trying to identify the colors of a specific breed, check the colors listed in the breed descriptions set forth by the various cat registries. Color descriptions may vary between registries, and different countries may also have different names for the colors.

The name of the color matters only if you are registering a pedigreed cat or entering a cat show with a breed in which there are color divisions; otherwise, it doesn't matter whether you call your cat gray or smoke or lilac. Your cat won't care, and because you love your cat, you won't care either.

It's always nice to adopt a stray cat or rescue a cat from a local shelter, but what if you have your heart set on certain characteristics in your cat? If you want a talkative breed, you might look for a Siamese or one of the other Asian breeds known to enjoy carrying on conversations. Maybe you've fallen in love with the ruddy coloration of an Abyssinian, or you want an athletic cat of any color. If your shelves are filled with treasured heirlooms, you may prefer a cat like the Ragdoll, who's not as likely to jump and climb. Perhaps you love the look of long, flowing fur or, at the opposite end of the spectrum, you find a hairless cat your ideal. These are all good reasons to consider a pedigreed cat.

You might be attracted to the idea of cat shows and decorating your walls with the ribbons your cat wins. Maybe you've even become so enthralled by a particular breed that you'd like to start your own cattery.

For any of the aforementioned reasons, you should look for your pedigreed cat from a breeder. Another reason you might want to get your cat from a breeder is that there are certain hereditary diseases in cats. If there are genetic tests for specific diseases, a reputable breeder will have had them done. You'll know that the mother cat (the queen) has had proper nourishment and necessary vaccinations. When you pick up your kitten, you'll know he's been wormed, if necessary, and had preliminary shots.

The Ragdoll is one of the more docile cat breeds.

When you buy from a breeder, you may get a written contract that states the purchase price and any conditions, like spaying or neutering the cat. There may be a health guarantee as well, stating that the cat is free of inherited diseases. There may also be a time frame during which you can return the kitten and receive your money back. Or the contract may state that if your kitten dies within a certain amount of time, the breeder will give you a replacement kitten.

While some breeders may not, a truly good breeder will agree to take back any cat she has bred at any time, and for any reason. This means that if a time comes when you can no longer care for your cat, you know that he will be returned to the breeder's care rather than end up in a shelter. The older I get, the more reassuring that kind of guarantee is.

Bengal cats have distinct tiger-like markings.

A Scottish Fold mother and kittens.

Another great thing about getting a cat from a breeder is that you've got someone to turn to for advice and information, whether you have a behavior question or you want to learn more about cat shows. Whatever your cat-related question, your breeder will be there for you.

In addition to the contract and a copy of your kitten's pedigree, the breeder may give you a small bag or can of whatever food your kitten is used to and maybe even a small bag of litter. At the very least, your breeder will tell you what kind of food she feeds and what kind of cat litter she uses.

When you begin your search for a pedigreed cat, understand that the closer your cat is to breed perfection, the more expensive he will be. Also, if you are particularly interested in breeding stock, an established breeder will have a lot of questions for you before she will sell you a cat that you intend to use for breeding. There will be additional contracts involved. Many breeders will sell unaltered cats only to other breeders. One breeder I know won't sell pet-quality cats until they are four to five months old and can be spayed or neutered before they go to their new homes.

Expect to pay from a few hundred to a few thousand dollars for a pedigreed cat, depending on the breed and the kitten's quality. Understand that quality is based on how closely the kitten meets the breed standard. A pet-quality cat who has some flaws according to the standard should still be a healthy cat. "Pet-quality" should never mean that a cat is sickly or deformed.

A great way to see many different breeds and to talk to people about their breeds is to attend a cat show. This will give you a chance to find out more about a breed before you invest in a cat. Don't be surprised if people are willing to talk but won't let you touch their cats. It's nothing personal.

Maine Coons are among the largest domesticated cats.

They just don't want germs spread from one cat to another. If they do let you pet their cats, don't be offended if they offer you hand sanitizer before they let you touch. They are protecting their cats.

You can find lists of breeders on the cat associations' websites. While a breeder's membership in an association does not guarantee her honesty or the quality of her cats, most breeders who join associations do so because they want to improve their breeds and produce the best cats possible.

BREEDER SEARCH

How to find breeders affiliated with the various cat registries:

- **Cat Fanciers Association:** Go to *www.cfa.org* and click on the Secure CFA tab to create an account and access the breeder referral service.

- **The International Cat Association:** Go to *www.tica.org* and click on Find a Kitten on the lefthand menu.

- **American Cat Fanciers Association:** Go to *www.acfacat.com* and click on Breed Directory.

- **Canadian Cat Association:** Go to *www.cca-afc.com*, click on Breeds, and then choose Breeders from the drop-down menu.

Maine coons have long, bushy tails and tufted paw pads.

Popular Cat Breeds 7

Here, we will take a closer look at some of the breeds that consistently rank among the most popular: the Abyssinian, American Shorthair, British Shorthair, Devon Rex, Exotic Shorthair, Maine Coon Cat, Persian, Ragdoll, Scottish Fold, Siamese, and Sphynx.

Abyssinian

The Abyssinian is an elegant, muscular cat that many people feel looks a bit like the African wildcat that is the common ancestor of domestic cats. It is believed that the breed originated along the Indian Ocean, in parts of Southeast Asia. The breed was refined in England, resulting in an elegant, intelligent companion.

Abyssinians are social, inquisitive, and constantly moving; they jump, climb, and explore. If you want a cat who can learn some

SOMALI
If everything about the Abyssinian sounds ideal, but you'd prefer a longhaired cat, consider the Somali, a longhaired breed that is the result of a recessive gene in the Abyssinian.

tricks, the Abyssinian is the cat for you. If you'd like a silent cat, however, keep looking; the Abyssinian is not shy about voicing his opinion.

Abyssinians weigh between 6 and 10 pounds (2.7–4.5 kg) and have a life span of between nine and fifteen years. They are often seen in a distinctive reddish color with darker ticking, but they also come in chocolate, cinnamon, blue, lilac, fawn, and a silver version of them all.

Abyssinians are healthy cats but they can develop a hereditary condition known as pyruvate kinase (PK) deficiency. This is caused by a recessive gene, and DNA testing can determine whether a cat is normal, a carrier, or affected by PK deficiency. A responsible breeder should test her cats before breeding.

Abyssinian

American Shorthair

The American Shorthair's ancestors probably came over to the United States on the Mayflower. This breed is an all-around good cat—generally healthy, agreeable to people of all ages and other pets, and talented as a rodent killer. These medium-sized cats weigh between 6 and 15 pounds (2.7–6.8 kg), with males on the larger end of the spectrum. The breed has a life span of fifteen to twenty years and a risk of hypertrophic cardiomyopathy (HCM).

British Shorthair

The British Shorthair is another good-sized cat, weighing between 8 and 20 pounds (3.6–9.1 kg), depending on whether you have a male or female; males are typically larger. This breed comes in many different colors and patterns and has an easygoing personality, generally getting along well with both adults and children. However, British Shorthairs aren't always happy being carried, so any children in the family should not make a habit of lugging the cat around. The British Shorthair can be a bit clumsy at times, so you should move priceless antiques to safe locations.

This is a generally healthy breed but is prone to HCM as well as hemophilia B, a hereditary bleeding disorder that can be identified with a DNA test. British Shorthairs can live from twelve to seventeen years. The British Longhair is the same breed, but with long hair.

Devon Rex

The Devon Rex has big ears, big eyes, and a big personality. A Devon Rex is always ready to play or just to help around the house with whatever chore you might be doing. Give him a ride on your shoulder or offer a cozy lap, and he's happy with that, too. If you are gone for long hours every day, consider a different breed because the Devon Rex is very social and likes company. The Devon also likes food and will not only clean his plate, but will also offer to help you with yours.

American Shorthair

British Shorthair

This 5- to 10-pound (2.3- to 4.5-kg) cat lives up to fifteen years, and the breed's coat ranges from wavy/curly to soft down. Health concerns include hypertrophic cardiomyopathy, patellar luxation, and hereditary myopathy. Make sure the breeder has screened breeding stock for hypertrophic cardiomyopathy and patellar luxation.

Exotic Shorthair

The Exotic Shorthair is basically a Persian with shorter hair. Developed by crossing Persians with American Shorthairs, with a dash of Burmese and Russian Blue, the Exotic has a thick, plush coat that doesn't mat or tangle and requires much less grooming than a Persian's long coat. Exotic Shorthairs come in all of the many colors of Persians, so you can have the added bonus of a cat in a color you prefer. An Exotic may be a bit more playful than a Persian, but if you love the sweet, round look and gentle, affectionate temperament of the Persian but don't want the chore of daily grooming, the Exotic is the cat for you.

Exotics have a lifespan of eight to fifteen years and weigh between 7 and 12 pounds (3.2–5.4 kg). Since Exotics may inherit polycystic kidney disease, ask the breeder if your prospective kitten's parents have been checked for cysts on the kidney.

Maine Coon Cat

The Maine Coon is the official cat of the state of Maine, where the breed's long coat, tufted ears, and large, well-furred paws make it well adapted to New England winters. This is a large, solidly built cat that weighs between 9 and 18 pounds (4.1–8.2 kg).

Devon Rex

Exotic Shorthair kitten

Maine Coon Cats are playful, affectionate, and social. They want to be where their people are. They also enjoy playing in water, so don't be surprised if you find a catnip mouse floating in your Maine Coon's water bowl.

Health issues include HCM, hip dysplasia, and spinal muscular atrophy (SMA). The Maine Coon Cat is the only cat breed affected by SMA, a disease caused by the death of spinal cord neurons, leading to muscle weakness and degeneration. Kittens with SMA have difficulty jumping and have a swaying gait, but they are not in pain and can live happy lives. Fortunately, there is a DNA test for this condition. There's also a test for the genetic mutation that causes HCM, so make sure that the breeder has tested both parents.

Persian

Persians are perfectly happy to play, but they aren't as into climbing and jumping as some other breeds. These affectionate cats enjoy being petted, and because their long, gorgeous fur makes people want to pet them, it's a win-win situation.

HIMALAYAN

The Himalayan is a colorpoint cat that is considered a color division of the Persian by the Cat Fanciers Association and as a separate breed by The International Cat Association and the American Cat Fanciers Association.

The drawback to that lovely coat is that Persians require daily grooming, particularly in the areas that are hard for a cat to reach when it self-grooms, such as the base of the ears and where the legs join the body.

These longhaired beauties come in more than eighty different color combinations and can live up to twenty years. There are two types of Persian: the traditional, or Doll Face, and the show Persian. While their coats and personalities are the same, the traditional

Maine Coon

Persian has a longer nose while the show Persian has a flat nose. Because of the flat nose, show Persians may have sinus problems or have trouble breathing, especially in hot weather. If you don't have air conditioning in your home, you should give your Persian a cool area to rest, even if it's just a cool tile floor.

Health problems in the breed can include polycystic kidney disease, progressive retinal atrophy, hypertrophic cardiomyopathy, bladder stones, bladder infections, and liver shunts.

Ragdoll

If you'd like a laid-back cat with no interest in climbing your bookcases or jumping onto your countertops, the Ragdoll may be just the cat for you. Developed in the 1960s by California breeder Ann Baker, the Ragdoll is a large cat (males can weigh up to 20 pounds [9.1 kg]) that makes a gentle companion. Ragdolls typically play without extending their claws, and they enjoy being around people. Ragdolls come in three color patterns: mitted, bicolor, and colorpoint, the latter of which allows for no white.

The Ragdoll matures slowly, taking about four years to reach full size. Because Ragdoll kittens can have rapid growth spurts, owners must make sure that they have plenty of food. If your young Ragdoll licks his plate clean, you should offer a little more food until he is full. Once your cat has stopped growing, you should determine a measured amount of food to keep him healthy but not fat.

Persian kitten

Ragdoll

Life expectancy for a Ragdoll is twelve to seventeen years. Health concerns include bladder stones and hypertrophic cardiomyopathy (HCM). There is a test to check for the genetic mutation that causes HCM, so make sure the breeder has tested both parents.

Scottish Fold

The first known Scottish Fold cat was a white barn cat named Susie, found in a litter in 1961 by William Ross, who went on to develop the breed. Susie's ears folded forward and down, and this trait, along with large, round eyes and a short nose, gives the Scottish Fold a look that somewhat resembles a cuddly owl. The Scottish Fold has a short, dense coat and, in temperament, is as sweet as he looks.

Kittens are born with upright ears that either stay straight or fold over around one month of age. Cats whose ears remain upright are known as Scottish Shorthairs. A longhaired variety is known as the Highland Fold.

Although the sweet look of a Scottish Fold is endearing, the upright-eared cats are essential to the health of the breed. When Folds are bred to Folds, the kittens may develop osteochondrodystrophy, a crippling and painful skeletal abnormality. A kitten with stiff legs or a short, thick tail may have osteochondrodystrophy.

Scottish Folds weigh between 8 and 13 pounds (3.6–5.9 kg) and have a lifespan of between eleven and fourteen years.

Siamese

Siamese cats are descended from the sacred temple cats of Siam (now Thailand). The first one in the United States arrived in 1878 when Rutherford B. Hayes and his wife, Lucy, received one as a gift from the American Consul in Bangkok.

Siamese are both independent and affectionate, with a habit of being very vocal. They have sleek coats and are instantly recognizable for having light-colored bodies with dark-colored legs, tails, ears, and faces. Siamese come in four recognized colors: seal,

Scottish Fold

Siamese

with a fawn body and almost black points; chocolate, with a cream body and milk-chocolate-colored points; blue point, with a bluish-white body and slate-blue points; and lilac point, with a white body and pinkish-gray points.

Siamese weigh between 6 and 10 pounds (2.7–4.5 kg) and come in show and traditional types. The show Siamese has a muscular, tubular body; long legs; a wedge-shaped head; and large, triangular ears. The traditional, or apple-headed, Siamese has a chunkier body and a rounded head.

With a life expectancy of eleven to fifteen years, the show type may be more prone to respiratory and dental problems. Other health concerns include bladder stones, glaucoma, progressive retinal atrophy, heart problems, and certain types of cancer. While some Siamese may have a kinked tail or crossed eyes, modern breeding practices have greatly eliminated these traits.

Sphynx

Many breeds begin with a spontaneous genetic mutation, and that's the case with the Sphynx, which began when a hairless kitten was born in 1966 in Toronto, Canada. While a Sphynx may have a bit of hair on the nose, ears, and tail, and may sometimes be covered in a fine down, generally, the Sphynx feels like a suede-covered hot water bottle. The skin is loose, so your Sphynx will look a bit wrinkled. All colors are possible in the breed.

Sphynx are lovable, energetic, mischievous, and generally happy to meet strangers. They use their toes almost like fingers when exploring new things.

While there's no long hair to brush, the Sphynx does need periodic bathing to help remove skin oils that hair would normally absorb. Start out young with your kitten to make sure he gets used to being bathed.

The Sphynx weighs between 6 to 12 pounds (2.7–5.4 kg) and has a life expectancy of eight to fourteen years. As with many other breeds, there's a danger of HCM and hereditary myopathy, a neurological disease that affects muscle function. The Sphynx may also develop skin conditions, such as urticaria pigmentosa or cutaneous mastocytosis. While any cat may develop periodontal disease, Sphynx seem especially susceptible, so start a tooth-brushing routine with your Sphynx starting in kittenhood.

Sphynx

Maybe you'd like a very different type of cat, one whose breed isn't easily recognized by most people. A rare-breed cat can be the perfect pet as long as you choose it for the traits it possesses, and not just because it's rare.

In alphabetical order, we'll discuss some rare cat breeds that you might consider: the American Bobtail, the American Wirehair, Balinese, Bombay, Burmilla, Havana Brown, Japanese Bobtail, Korat, LaPerm, Peterbald, Ragamuffin, and Turkish Van.

American Bobtail

The American Bobtail is a moderately large cat, with males weighing between 12 and 16 pounds (5.4–7.3 kg), and females ranging from 7 to 11 pounds (3.2–5.0 kg). They come in all colors and patterns, and may have short or medium-long coats. As the name implies, the American Bobtail has a naturally bobbed tail. The tail can range in size, but it never reaches beyond the hock joint of the rear leg.

American Wirehair

American Bobtails are muscular cats whose hind legs are longer than their front legs. They are friendly and intelligent and will happily greet adults, children, and any canine family members. They love to play games, including fetch and hide-and-seek. They are also easily leash-trained, which is a desirable trait if you'd like to take your cat for walks.

The American Bobtail is a healthy breed, but cats that are totally tailless can have spinal problems that affect their ability to control defecation. Their life span is from eleven to fifteen years.

American Wirehair

The American Wirehair is the result of a spontaneous mutation that was first seen in a litter in 1966. While there are some physical differences besides the coat, the American Wirehair is similar to the American Shorthair, and breeding one to the other is allowed.

American Bobtail

The wiry coat defines this breed and comes in degrees of wiriness, from spiked to curly. Individual hairs, including the whiskers, may be crimped, hooked, or bent. They need very little grooming because a brush or comb can damage the coat, but occasional bathing to remove dead hair is a good idea to prevent loose, hooked hairs from irritating the skin.

American Wirehairs are quiet, loving cats, a bit on the reserved side. They weigh between 6 and 11 pounds (2.7–5.0 kg) and have a lifespan of fourteen to eighteen years. The breed is generally healthy but may develop hypertrophic cardiomyopathy (HCM).

Balinese

The Balinese is essentially a longhaired Siamese, the result of a spontaneous mutation. Breeders began breeding for this type in the 1950s. There is no undercoat, so the breed's long, flowing fur is easy to care for and unlikely to mat. The Balinese comes in traditional Siamese colors as well as nontraditional colors such as tabby point and tortie point.

Like the Siamese, the Balinese is curious and mischievous as well as affectionate. He enjoys talking, but his voice is a bit softer and less insistent than that of a Siamese. This longhaired beauty weighs between 5 and 10 pounds (2.3–4.5 kg) and has a life expectancy of nine to fifteen years. He may develop heart problems and can be affected by lysomomal storage disease.

Bombay

This black cat brings good luck in the form of a loving, playful pet who wants to be with his people. If you want a loving companion, the Bombay fits the bill.

The Bombay is the result of a Kentucky breeder, Nikki Horner, who wanted to produce a domestic cat that looked like the wild Indian panther. She started by crossing a black American Shorthair with a sable (rich solid brown) Burmese. The end result was a solid black cat with mesmerizing eyes. The Bombay sports a gorgeous, sleek black coat and glowing eyes that range from gold to copper.

Balinese

Bombay

Burmilla

Bombays weigh between 6 and 11 pounds (2.7–5.0 kg) and have a life expectancy of twelve to sixteen years. Like so many cats, they are susceptible to HCM and, because of their short muzzles, may have breathing difficulties.

Burmilla

The name Burmilla is taken from the names of the two breeds in its background: the Burmese and the Chinchilla Persian. (*Note:* Some consider the Chinchilla Persian to be a separate breed; others consider chinchilla a silvery color variation.) The result is a medium-sized cat with a silvery coat that may be tipped or shaded with black, brown, lilac, blue, chocolate, cream, red, or tortoiseshell. The coat may be short or semi-long. Burmillas have distinctive black "eyeliner" around their eyes, lips, and noses. Another striking feature is their eyes, which may be any shade of green. Their color changes as they age, so you won't know your cat's permanent color until he is fully grown.

Burmillas get along well with children and other pets and are gentle, playful, and loving. These sweet cats weigh between eight and ten pounds and have a life expectancy of ten to fifteen years. They can be prone to allergies and may develop polycystic kidney disease.

Havana Brown

If you love chocolate, or maybe a good cigar, the Havana Brown may be your soul mate. British breeders who wanted to create a brown cat developed this cat. They crossed Siamese with black domestic shorthairs, eventually resulting in the Havana Brown— named, some say, after the color of a Havana cigar. Other distinguishing features are the breed's green eyes, forward-tilting ears, and a "corncob" muzzle shape. The International Cat Association (TICA) allows a lilac (pinkish-gray) color and, upon accepting that color, changed the breed's name to simply Havana.

No matter what you call him, the Havana Brown is a cat who wants to be with you and supervise whatever you're doing. He explores with his paws and enjoys talking. Don't get a Havana Brown if you're usually gone all day; this cat is much too social for that.

Havana Browns weigh between 6 and 10 pounds (2.7–4.5 kg) and have a life expectancy of ten to fifteen years. This is a healthy breed but may be prone to developing stones in the urinary tract.

Japanese Bobtail

The Japanese Bobtail is a loving, friendly breed that enjoys a game of fetch and is a good candidate for agility. The breed has been known in Japan for hundreds of years but first appeared in the United States in the late 1900s, where it is still relatively rare. Its most distinguishing feature is its bobtail, and no two tails are ever alike. Its hind legs are longer than its front legs, and it comes in shorthaired and longhaired varieties.

Japanese Bobtails come in solid colors, bicolor, vans, and calicos (called *mi-ke* in Japan). While more bicolored and van-patterned Bobtails are registered in the United States, the calico is considered the luckiest color in Japan—although any Bobtail is thought of as lucky and able to bring prosperity and happiness to his owner. The popular type of statue called *maneki neko*, or "beckoning cat," is a Bobtail, and many Japanese shopkeepers have these statues in their stores to attract good people.

Japanese Bobtails weigh between 6 and 10 pounds (2.7–4.5 kg) and have a life expectancy of nine to fifteen years. They have no major health problems, and the gene associated with the short tail does not produce any spinal abnormalities.

Havana
Brown

Japanese Bobtail

Korat

The Korat of Thailand is another cat that is considered good luck. His fur is said to glisten like silver; his green eyes symbolize prosperity; and his heart-shaped face brings happiness to brides. If there's a kink in his tail, the luck increases. The Korat can be a real cuddle cat; he likes being with his human family and he has a playful streak.

The Korat comes in only one color: a silver-tipped blue. The coat is short and lies close to the body. The breed does not attain its distinctive green eye color until between the ages of two and four, and this slow-maturing cat is not fully developed physically or emotionally until he is five years old.

This gentle cat weighs between 6 and 10 pounds (2.7–4.5 kg) and has a life expectancy of ten to fifteen years. He is prone to a fatal genetic condition, the GM-1 and GM-2 gangliosidoses (also known as lysosomal storage disease), but breeders can test their breeding stock to identify carriers, so your breeder should be able to guarantee your Korat's health.

Korat

LaPerm

The LaPerm is a curious, active cat who loves heights, whether it's your shoulder or the top shelf of a bookcase. That doesn't mean he doesn't also appreciate a lap for snuggling, which is lucky for the owner, because the curly LaPerm coat just cries out for you to bury your fingers in it.

The distinctive coat is the result of a spontaneous mutation first seen in 1982. LaPerms come in any color or pattern and may have long or short hair. The longhaired variety is sometimes called a "gypsy shag." Both long- and shorthaired varieties have kinked whiskers.

A LaPerm kitten can be born bald or may go bald at about two weeks of age, with the coat finally growing back by about four months of age. If a kitten is born with a straight coat, either he will shed that coat in exchange for a curly one, or the coat will stay straight. Kittens born with curly coats will always have curly coats.

Female LaPerms weigh between 5 and 8 pounds (2.3–3.6 kg), and males weigh between 8 and 10 pounds (3.6–4.5 kg). Life expectancy is ten to fifteen years. The LaPerm has no known genetic diseases.

Peterbald

The Peterbald is originally from Russia, where it was first named the Don Sphynx. Later developments of the breed in St. Petersburg let to the name Peterbald. This very rare breed was accepted in 2005 by TICA. The Cat Fanciers Association (CFA) does not recognize it as a breed.

The Peterbald is very affectionate and friendly as well as a bit talkative. Enormous ears that look as though they could lift the cat right off the ground with one flap top his wedge-shaped head.

The Peterbald comes in five coat types: straight, naked, chamois, flock, and brush. The straight is a full shorthaired coat, but, while cats with this type of coat may be bred, they are not eligible for the show ring. Naked Peterbalds have no fur—just soft, warm skin. Chamois cats have a suede, or "peach-fuzz," texture. Flock-coated cats have a fine, velvety coat, and cats with brush coats have sparse, wiry coats that are irregular in texture.

Like all hairless, or mostly hairless, breeds, your Peterbald may appreciate a sweater or access to a soft blanket in cold weather. Also limit his exposure to sunlight because he can get sunburned.

LaPerm

Peterbald kitten

The Ragamuffin is a large cat, weighing between 10 and 20 pounds (4.5–9.1 kg), with a life expectancy of twelve to sixteen years. Health issues include HCM and polycystic kidney disease. The Ragamuffin is also prone to periodontal disease.

Turkish Van

The Turkish is a strong, agile cat who loves running, jumping (to the highest shelf he can reach), and playing in water. Unlike many cats, the Turkish Van enjoys water and is sometimes called the swimming cat. He's affectionate in that he will follow you from room to room, and he won't mind being petted, but he is not a cuddle cat and would prefer not to be held.

Females weigh between 6 and 8 pounds (2.7–3.6 kg), with males between 8 and 10 pounds (3.6–4.5 kg). Life expectancy is between twelve and fifteen years. The gene that causes hairlessness may also cause feline ectodermal dysplasia, which can cause missing and/or malformed teeth.

Ragamuffin

The Ragamuffin is a low-maintenance, gentle cat who is very tolerant of children, loves to be near people, and, like the Ragdoll, may totally relax and go limp in your arms. The Ragamuffin's coat is medium-long and comes in all colors and patterns. Cats with colorpoints may be registered but not shown. The breed is recognized by the CFA but not TICA.

Ragamuffin

Turkish Van

The Turkish Van is considered a regional treasure and was possibly named after Lake Van in Turkey. The van color pattern comes from the distinctive color markings of the Turkish Van, consisting of color on primarily the head and tail. These patches were originally seen in rich red but can be any solid color. Turkish Vans can also be solid white, sometimes called Van Kedi.

The Turkish Van takes three to five years to mature, with an average weight of between 10 and 18 pounds (4.5–8.2 kg). Their life expectancy is between twelve and seventeen years, and they have no specific health problems.

DID YOU KNOW?

The Exotic Shorthair has a funny nickname—he's often called "the lazy man's Persian" because he shares the Persian's adorable face, but his short, plush coat is not nearly as high-maintenance.

9 Adopting Your Cat

If you want a pet cat and are not concerned about breed or pedigree, getting a cat from a friend or neighbor can be a good option. If that friend's or neighbor's cat has kittens, then you'll be getting a youngster who will come to you with no bad habits and, hopefully, no diseases. You will have met the mother and will know what her temperament is like. If she's calm and friendly, chances are that her kittens will be that way, too.

If you are adopting an older cat from someone you know, some of the same principles hold true. You'll know how old the cat is, you'll know what kind of personality the cat has, and you can ask the owner about vaccinations, medications, and health issues. If you have children or a dog, you may also have an idea of how the cat will interact with them.

Getting a cat from your local animal shelter or rescue is also a very good way to get a cat, and there are always plenty of cats in need of good homes. While a shelter cat's exact age may be unknown, he will have been checked by the shelter veterinarian and be up to date on vaccinations, free of fleas and ticks, and spayed or neutered. The shelter may also have implanted a microchip for identification purposes. If the cat was surrendered, the former owner may have given the shelter some personality and behavior information, such as if the cat is good around children and other pets. From observing and interacting with the cat, the shelter staff will likely know whether the cat is a cuddler, is very active, is vocal, and other traits.

If you have your heart set on a kitten, check your local shelter in the spring. Most shelters are inundated with pregnant cats and kittens each spring. You'll have your pick of just about every color and coat length. Many shelters perform early spay/neuters. If not, they might offer a voucher for a free or reduced-cost spay/neuter when the kitten is a bit older.

Many cats await loving homes in local animal shelters.

You might adopt a kitten
from a friend or neighbor.

10 Considering a Stray

A stray cat usually returns to places where he has found food.

There are several things to think about if you want to take in a stray cat. First, there are different kinds of stray cats. *Feral cats* are domestic cats that have "gone wild." Maybe they were born and have lived their entire lives outdoors, or maybe they once lived in homes but have been in the "wild" for so long that they've adopted wild behavior.

Most feral cats avoid human contact. Although they may approach homes where they are fed, they frequently will wait until they are alone before eating. Many people feed feral cats, gradually trapping them, spaying or neutering, and then releasing them back into their colony.

Feral cats help control the rodent population, especially in cities.

Helping to maintain feral cats can be rewarding, and the cats can be fun to watch, but feral cats can be very hard to tame. You have a better chance of raising the cat to be a pet if you take in a feral cat as a kitten but, even then, there's no guarantee. Friends of mine took in a feral kitten, but he had already missed the critical socialization period, and he grew wilder and wilder, frequently biting and scratching with no provocation.

A stray cat who has started to hang out by your kitchen door is another story. A cat who is happy to be

RABIES
Consider that a stray cat may not have been vaccinated against rabies, and a stray is more likely to encounter wild animals that may be rabid.

around people and might actually enter the house when invited is a stray who, for one reason or another, no longer has a home.

Many people adopt, or are adopted by, stray cats. If you're not looking for any particular character traits and you don't mind not knowing exactly how old the cat is, this is a perfectly good way to get a cat, but there are many unknowns that you'll need to consider. With a stray, you don't know the cat's health history. For example, there's no way to tell if the cat has been vaccinated, and the stray may have feline leukemia, feline immunodeficiency virus, or feline panleukopenia (feline distemper). Because this is your first cat, you don't need to worry about the stray infecting a resident cat, but you don't know if that stray is ill or likely to become ill. You also may be opening your door to fleas and ticks as well as the cat.

While a veterinarian can make an educated guess about the cat's age, you won't know the exact age of your new family member. And, with a stray, you won't know just what kind of a personality he has, even if he's a pedigreed cat.

Our neighbors have a beautiful cat they took in as a stray. She is not a cuddler, and she rarely, if ever, sits on a lap. Her family is fine with that, and they love her, but if you want overt affection from a cat, maybe you should say no to a stray.

Some diseases that infect cats can be transmitted to people, and stray cats have a higher risk of contracting these diseases. Toxoplasmosis is one of these. Toxoplasmosis is generally not a problem for humans other than pregnant women. Because the disease is transmitted through cat feces, pregnant women are advised not to clean litter boxes. This doesn't mean that you can't have a cat if you're pregnant; it means that someone else gets litter-box duties. However, if someone in the household is pregnant, taking in a stray is not your best option for getting a cat.

Bartonellosis, or "cat scratch fever," is transmitted to cats by fleas. While not serious in healthy humans, it can cause problems in people with compromised immune systems. Keeping a cat flea-free is a good preventative, and a stray may already have a flea infestation.

None of the foregoing means that you shouldn't welcome a stray. It does mean that, if you've made the decision to keep a stray, you should take him to a veterinarian sooner rather than later.

You have a better chance of raising a happy pet if you adopt a stray as a kitten.

PART II

When Kitty Comes Home

First Day at Home 11

If you're getting an adult cat, some of this information about a cat's first day at home won't apply. What *will* apply is that your house is strange to your new cat, and there may be a period of adjustment. Whether you're bringing home an adult or a kitten, be patient and let him get used to all of the new things he's encountering.

There's some truth to the old adage "curiosity killed the cat," so before you introduce your cat or kitten to your home, do some "cat-proofing." Make sure that electrical cords are either tight against the baseboards or encased in a length of PVC pipe. Vertical, rather than horizontal, blinds will help deter unwanted climbing. Most blinds no longer have looped cords and have sticks to twist them open and closed, but if

you have older blinds, snip the cords so your cat can't get caught in them. Move heavy books to the bottom shelves of bookcases so that leaping cats can't topple them; you also might consider securing bookcases to the walls.

All cats like hiding places, but some hiding places can be dangerous. If you have a reclining chair, always check to make sure that your cat isn't hiding in its depths. Activating the reclining mechanism can seriously injure your cat. Other places that can turn into death traps for your cat are washing machines, clothes dryers, refrigerators, freezers, and dishwashers. Cats are quick and can be silent, so before you use any of these appliances, check that your cat is not inside.

Welcome your new cat with affection, but remember to give him his space, too.

Keep in mind that cats can squeeze into small spaces to hide.

Cats also seem to love hiding in box springs. If there's a small tear in your mattress, for example, your cat may open it further and crawl inside. While box springs don't pose an immediate threat, your cat could get tangled in the springs, so it's a good idea to repair any openings in furniture.

When planning to bring home a new kitten or cat, try to do it when someone will be home all day. Get him on a Friday night, for instance, so that you'll have two days to help him get adjusted before everyone goes back to school or work.

While crates are typically thought of in connection with dogs, a crate can work for a kitten, too. The enclosed space will make him feel more secure and, when you're not watching him, the crate will keep him safe and away from electrical wires and other potential dangers. If you decide to use a crate, a fiberglass one may be a better choice than a wire one, especially for a kitten, who might be able to squeeze between the bars. If you don't want to use a crate, a large cardboard box or a plastic storage bin without the lid can work as a temporary bed.

Whatever you use, keep it in a quiet place, like a spare bedroom, where your kitten can rest undisturbed.

Keep the atmosphere at home relatively calm. This is not the time to invite all of your friends and relatives to meet the kitten; let him get used to you and the other members of the household first. Certainly, children should pet and hold him—just not your child's entire class!

Show your kitten the litter box and supervise his first few trips there to make sure that he knows where it is. Even if you're planning on eventually keeping the litter box in the basement, keep it on the house's main floor in the beginning. Kittens are too small to easily navigate stairs. Yes, cats instinctively search out dirt, but don't make that search impossible.

Kittens are curious and adaptable, and it won't be long before your new kitten has settled in and eagerly explored every area of your (and his!) home.

If you use a crate with your cat, a fiberglass crate is recommended.

HOME FOR THE HOLIDAYS?

The belief used to be that Christmas was the absolute worst time to get a pet of any kind; however, the San Francisco SPCA has found that the number of animals returned after being adopted at Christmastime is no greater than at other times of the year. There are many reasons why the winter holidays may still not be the best time. If your house is "holiday central" for all of the relatives, or if you always host the neighborhood party, maybe it's best to wait on getting a kitten or cat. Likewise, if you have very young children, it might be better to wait. Children can get pretty wound up around holiday time, and your new pet needs relative calm so he can adjust to all of the newness with a minimum of stress.

12 Meeting the Kids

There's nothing cuter than a kid and a kitten, but children—especially young ones—need to be supervised when they are with the new kitten or cat. A child doesn't always understand that he or she may be hurting a kitten, so it's up to you to keep all parties safe. Don't let your children sit on the cat, pull his ears or tail, or poke his eyes.

Pay attention to your cat. If his ears are back, his tail is thrashing, or he's hissing or growling, he's had enough. Remove him from the situation. Don't let children interfere with your cat when he is eating or sleeping. Crating your cat or putting him in a room by himself will give everyone a chance to calm down.

Encourage your children to sit on the floor to play with the cat or kitten and teach them the proper way to pick up the kitten: with one hand under the chest and the other supporting the hindquarters. Also, remember that, while an adult cat may have learned to play nicely, with claws sheathed, a kitten is more likely to scratch. Supervise playtime. Encourage using toys on poles so that the kitten's claws connect with feathers or fur, not skin. You don't want your child to get hurt.

Another good way to help strengthen the bond between your children and the kitten is to let them help take care of him. Even a small child can fill a water dish or scoop food from a can. Remember, though, that even though your children may enjoy caring for the kitten, it's up to you to make sure that the kitten isn't neglected because the children forgot or were too busy.

If you don't have children at home, but children visit from time to time, it's a good idea to introduce your kitten to some children. You want him to grow up to be a cat who is comfortable around both adults and children. Maybe there are some neighborhood children who'd like to meet your kitten. Just remember to supervise all interaction. You want this to be a positive experience for both the kitten and the children.

If you're adopting an older cat from a shelter or rescue, the volunteers may be able to tell you whether he is good with children, but maybe not. Always err on the side of caution. Make introductions slowly. Make sure the child understands to move slowly and quietly. The best way to make the introduction is for the child to sit quietly and let the cat come to him or her.

Make introductions with the child sitting on the floor.

No matter if you bring home a kitten or an adult cat, you must teach your children to handle the new pet gently.

If you have a dog, you can't just turn a cat—and definitely not a kitten—loose in the house and expect everyone to live happily ever after. At least an adult cat has a better chance at reaching safety than a kitten, and an adult cat might even stop a dog in his tracks by using his claws.

If you're introducing a kitten to your dog, put the kitten in a cat carrier for the initial introduction. Let the dog and kitten sniff each other through the carrier door. It may be that your dog is friendly and curious, and that's a good thing. If your dog tries to get to the kitten through the carrier, the introductions will take much longer.

Next, set your kitten up with his own bed, litter box, and food in a spare room with the door closed. Both the kitten and the dog will be able to smell each other through the crack under the door. When you want to let the kitten explore the house, crate your dog.

After a day or two, depending on the size of your dog, you might be able to put a baby gate in the doorway of the cat's room. The two pets can see and smell each other, but the kitten will be safe. Always supervise all contact until you are sure that they are safe together.

Take introductions slowly before you let your dog and kitten loose together.

With an adult cat, things can be both easier and more complicated. An adult cat may or may not already be familiar with dogs. You'll still want that safe area for the cat, but adult cats have full use of their claws and are faster and more able to get to that safe area.

Use baby gates wherever necessary so that your cat can leap over, leaving the dog behind. Clear a shelf or two and remove things from your fireplace mantel so that the cat always has someplace high and safe where he can rest undisturbed. Keep the litter box in a room that is a "dog-free" zone. Again, a baby gate across the doorway may work. It's not fair to your cat to have to try to use the litter box while a dog is present, especially if the two are not yet best buddies. It's a good idea to keep the litter box where the dog can't get at it anyway because many dogs seem to find litter box deposits tasty.

Be patient. Total acceptance is not likely to happen in just a day or two. It can take weeks. Make sure neither animal can harass the other when you're not around. Supervise their meetings and praise both animals when they are calm and nonthreatening. Many dogs and cats become good friends, but even a truce can work as long as there are safety zones for everyone.

If you love having a cat and want another, follow a similar plan for meet-and-greets. A kitten in a carrier may be introduced initially to an adult cat. Then, as previously discussed, set up the safe room for the new cat or kitten and let the two cats smell each other at the crack under the door. When one cat has the run of the house, the other is confined. Also, when you've removed the new cat from his room to a safe place, let the resident cat check out the new cat's room. Having a diffuser of synthetic cat pheromones may also help relax the cats.

If the cats seem comfortable sniffing near the door, prop the door open a couple of inches and let them interact at that opening. If either cat seems stressed, end the session. Be patient with this process.

With careful introductions and supervision, your cat and dog can become best friends.

Eventually, enlist a helper and have the cats in the same room, but at opposite ends. Offer tasty treats and attention, especially if the cats are calm and ignoring each other. Gradually bring them closer and closer. Even if they never become best friends, it's good enough if they tolerate each other with no aggression. As mentioned in discussing introductions to dogs, have a cleared-off shelf or two where the cats can get away from each other.

If you have other types of pets, such as rabbits, gerbils, or hamsters, it's likely that they will never be friends with your cat. Your cat will see these animals as prey, so make sure that these other pets are in safe cages out of your cat's reach. If you have an aquarium, make sure that the lid is secure. Yes, there are cute videos online of cats cuddling with rabbits or a mouse perched on a cat's head, but these are not the norm. Keep all of your pets safe.

DID YOU KNOW?
While dogs are usually predictable in their behavior, cats are more independent and "creative" in their life skills.

Your dog and cat might not become cuddle buddies, but they can learn to coexist peacefully.

Kittens begin socializing from birth by interacting with their littermates.

Socialization is a term that you may associate more with dogs than with cats, but for any animal living with humans, socializing can ease stress and make life more pleasant for all parties. Here's an example with the wolves at the Wolf Park canid research and education facility in Battle Ground, Indiana. The wolves are handled daily from the time they are born, and the staff uses rewards to teach the wolves to allow, and enjoy, human contact. That means that when a wolf needs veterinary care, he is calm and unafraid around the staff and the veterinarian, and he doesn't need to be sedated or restrained for treatment.

While that's an extreme example, the principle is the same for your cat. The more people and things that your cat safely encounters as a kitten, the calmer, happier, and less stressed he will be in strange situations as an adult.

Many animals are touchy about having their feet handled, and cats are no exception. After all, a cat with an injured paw or leg is not going to be able to hunt effectively or to escape enemies. Gently handle your kitten's paws. Touch each one. Speak softly and offer tiny treats. Little bits of deli turkey are popular with most cats. Practice applying

Gentle petting and handling help socialize a kitten to humans.

gentle pressure to extend the claws. If your kitten resists, don't force the issue—just try again later.

When your kitten is OK with having his paws handled, try to clip a nail or two. Stop while your kitten is still relaxed—"make haste slowly" is the rule. Eventually, you should be able to clip his nails without a major fight.

Check your kitten's ears and acclimate him to having his ears touched. This may come in handy if you ever have to administer ear drops.

Also accustom your kitten to being held gently but firmly. Slide your hand under the kitten, with your hand cradling his body, a couple of fingers between his front legs, and the other fingers around his body. When he's bigger, use your other hand to support his

hindquarters. Have other people hold and handle your kitten, too. You want him to accept strangers handling him. It will make veterinary visits much more pleasant.

As previously discussed, show children the proper way to hold and pet a cat. Teach them not to pull the cat's tail or poke his ears or eyes.

Try not to step on your cat. That may sound obvious, but kittens and small cats aren't always on a person's radar, and a cat who gets stepped on may start to distrust all humans and decide that the best offense is a good defense.

Let your cat explore safely. You might not want him walking across your kitchen counter, but put away the breakables and let him wander the mantel or climb the bookcase as long as it's stable and in no danger of falling over when a cat's weight hits it. If your cat is still a kitten, definitely supervise. You don't want a kitten getting trapped someplace or getting injured.

Cats tend to be neglected when it comes to veterinary appointments. That's because, frequently, cats are hard to transport. Many dogs like car rides, or can at least be lifted into the car without too much struggle, but cats tend to protest, often in the form of claws out and fangs bared. Get your kitten used to a carrier when he is young. If you've adopted an adult cat, follow the same procedure. It may take a bit longer with an adult than with a kitten, so be patient.

Put a comfy blanket or pillow in the carrier and set the carrier on a chair or table.

Most cats like high places, so your cat may be more inclined to explore, and enter, the carrier if it's not on the floor. If your kitten is too young or too small to safely climb up to the carrier, leave the carrier on the floor. If you can remove the carrier door, do it; otherwise, fasten it so that it can't accidentally close on the cat.

Feed your cat in the carrier. If you feed both wet and dry cat food, feed the wet food only in the carrier. If your cat enjoys a particular treat, offer it only in the carrier. At intervals during the day, you might even lure your cat into the carrier with a small piece of deli turkey.

Do this for at least two weeks, or longer if needed. You're the best judge of when to move on to the next step, but remember that this is a slow process. Rushing it will only postpone the desired results.

When your cat seems completely comfortable in and around the carrier, shut the door while the cat is eating. Open it and let the cat out as soon as he has finished his meal. Gradually increase the time he's in the carrier with the door closed. You can offer him treats through the door grate to help keep him calm. While your cat may never love the carrier, he should at least be willing to get into it, making any car trip

Be prepared for your cat to climb, and keep his safety in mind.

more pleasant. If he panics at any time, you've gone too fast, so back up a little in your training.

Many veterinary clinics are trying to make their practices "fear free" for the animals they treat. While this is not necessarily a part of socialization, anything you can do to make your cat feel less stressed while at the veterinarian's office is a good thing. Take along some of that deli turkey, which may help distract your cat from the unknown of the waiting room, surrounded by strange cats and dogs.

When you visit the vet, bring a towel, a small blanket, or a rubber-backed mat to put on the exam table. That cold stainless-steel tabletop, with nothing for claws to grab onto, can make your cat insecure and frightened. A towel from home can help him feel calmer, while a rubber-backed mat will prevent him from slipping or sliding. Whatever you use, don't bring it out just for a veterinary visit. Place the towel or mat on one of your cat's favorite perches in the house. That way, it will smell like home, which can also reduce stress.

Trips to the vet's office don't have to be stressful.

In some cities and towns, cats don't need licenses like dogs do, but if your area requires rabies shots, you may need to attach your cat's rabies tag to a collar. If your cat is an indoor/outdoor cat, you might also want a tag with your contact information on it so that your cat can be returned to you if he gets lost. Some owners also like to put a bell on their outdoor cat's collar so that birds can hear him coming.

If you decide that you want your cat to have a collar, choose a breakaway collar or one that stretches. Cats, when outdoors, tend to stay close to shelter, such as bushes. They may also enjoy jumping over fences or squeezing through tight places. All of these activities mean that something could catch on your cat's collar, trapping him. A breakaway collar or one with an elastic insert means that your cat can pull out of the collar and get free.

Even if your cat is an indoors-only cat, there's always the chance that someone will leave a door or window open, and your cat could escape. Consider getting your cat microchipped. A microchip is a tiny insert the size of a grain of rice that contains a number exclusive to your cat. It's implanted under the skin, usually between the shoulders. You then register the chip with the company that made it, giving them your contact information.

A scanner can read the number on the microchip, and there are universal scanners that can read chips made by many different companies. Many animal shelters, veterinary clinics, and police departments have scanners, so whoever reads the chip can get in touch with the chip company who can contact you.

A collar can hold your cat's ID tag and rabies tag.

PART III

About Cat Behavior

It's amazing what you can find when you start snooping around the Internet, and theories about purring are a great example. Wikipedia says that there are many animals that purr in addition to cats, including raccoons, mongooses, bears, badgers, foxes, hyenas, rabbits, squirrels, guinea pigs, tapirs, lemurs, and gorillas.

Not all cats purr. Some cats roar. No cat can do both. Most smaller cats purr, and most large cats roar. Supposedly, the big cats can roar because their hyoid bone is incompletely ossified. Purring cats have a completely ossified hyoid bone. The exception to this is the snow leopard, who has an incompletely ossified hyoid bone but can't roar; while it does make a sound that's similar to purring, it is not a true purr.

While we tend to think of purring as that lovely "running motor" sound we hear when our cat is contented, a cat may purr for other reasons. A cat may purr because he's nervous, or he may purr as a way to signal to another animal that he is not a threat.

Some cats purr as a signal that they are hungry. A hungry purr and a contented purr have a different sound, and if your cat does both, you'll soon be able to tell the difference.

Cats also purr when in pain. Purrs have a frequency of around 25 Hz, and this frequency causes related vibrations in the body, which can improve bone density and promote healing. This frequency can also ease breathing and lessen pain and swelling.

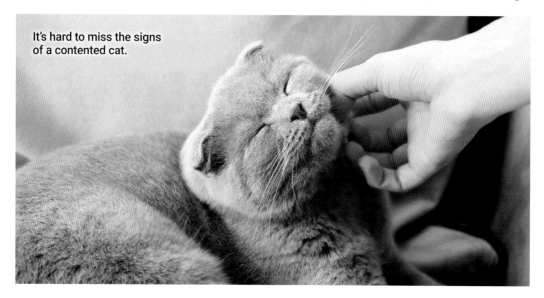

It's hard to miss the signs of a contented cat.

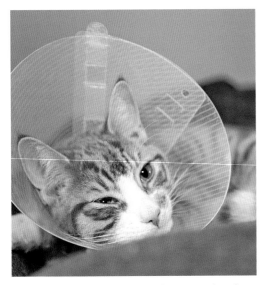

A cat makes a different-sounding purr when he is in distress.

So, while it's lovely to have a purring cat curled up in your lap, if your cat is purring and it seems out of context, make sure he's not in distress or injured.

Besides purring, when a cat is happy and relaxed and feeling safe, he may knead with his front paws, extending and retracting his claws. Many cat owners call this "making biscuits." Sometimes a cat will knead a pillow or a toy, but frequently he'll choose your lap. If your cat chooses the lap of a visitor, he's accepting that person. Besides showing that your cat is relaxed, kneading is also a way that your cat marks you as "his," leaving his scent from the scent glands in his toes. Keeping your cat's nails trimmed will make kneading less painful for you.

A cat also shows affection and marks you with his scent by cheek rubbing, which is often combined with head butting. If your cat would like some attention, he may butt his head against your chin, sometimes combining that with cheek rubbing. And, while you may not appreciate your cat rubbing back and forth on your legs when you're trying to bring in the groceries, your cat is greeting you and letting you know he's glad you're home.

Don't ignore the signs that your cat is unhappy.

Getting your first cat may mean that you don't know the physical signs that can indicate an unhappy cat. As an example, you may be stroking your cat gently and notice that his tail has begun to twitch back and forth. With a dog, a wagging tail is generally a sign of a happy dog. With a cat, a waving tail means the cat is agitated. In the case of stroking your cat, cats seem to have a lower threshold of enjoyment than dogs do. Dogs may let you pet them for as long as you're willing, but cats tend to like petting in small doses, and then they become uncomfortable. That twitching tail is a sign that your cat would like you to stop. If your cat's ears are pressed flat against his skull, then it *really* is time to stop.

Cats hiss for various reasons. Your cat may hiss if you startle him, or that hiss can mean "back off!" You may hear a hiss if you get too close and your cat thinks you might step on him. He may hiss if you bring a strange animal into the house. He may even hiss at people he doesn't know. It's a warning to not come any closer.

If you've never heard a cat growl, you'll be amazed at how menacing it sounds. It's hard to believe that such a low, throaty growl could come from that previously adorable kitty. The ominous rumble definitely means "hands off."

Don't try to pick up or touch a growling cat. Leave him alone for a while. If you must pick up your cat when he is—to put it bluntly—seriously pissed off, wear gloves and wrap him in a blanket.

Eventually, you will know your own cat. You'll know what makes him happy and what annoys him. It bears repeating that cats are not small dogs. When a dog rolls over, it generally means that he's looking for a good tummy rub. Your cat may also enjoy a gentle skritch on the tummy, but a cat on his back is also in a defensive position. This position allows him to use all four clawed paws, plus his teeth, and if your hand is in the middle, it's going to hurt. Until you know just what your cat means by rolling over, use caution when scratching his stomach.

Your cat's tail is indicative of his mood.

A cat's curiosity certainly extends to the kitchen.

Cats love to explore, and they love heights. If your cat will have free run of all counters, work surfaces, and tables, and your furniture will be just a giant cat playground, you can skip this section, but, if you'd like to have certain surfaces in your home cat-free, keep reading.

Kitchen counters seem to be an area that many cat owners would like to keep clear of cats. Unfortunately, there are usually good food smells on the counters that tempt even the best-mannered felines. Teaching your cat to stay off the kitchen counter is hard because cats like high places and, in the world of cats, they defer to the highest-ranking cat—but, if that cat isn't using a particular bed or perch, it's perfectly fine for another cat to use it. If you catch your cat on the counter, and he immediately jumps off, it's not because he "knows he's been bad." It's because you're the "highest-ranking cat," and if you want the counter, your cat is happy to oblige.

First, try to keep food off the counters when you're not actually preparing a meal. Second, be consistent, and make sure everyone in the family is consistent. If the counter is going to be out of bounds to your cat, say "no" and take him off the counter every single time you catch him there. If one person thinks it's cute and lets him stay up there just one time, your cat has learned that it's OK, no matter how many times the rest of the family picks him up and tells him "no."

A climbing cat will be happy to help himself to a tasty treat.

Squirting your cat with water can work, but you have to be there to catch him and squirt him, so that won't work when your cat is home alone and likely to cruise the countertops. If you don't think he's up there when no one's home, dust your countertop with a light layer of flour before you leave the house. Chances are, when you return, there'll be paw prints in the flour.

Putting something on the counter surface to deter the cat is another popular option. Put double-sided tape or sticky furniture strips (made for cats to discourage scratching) on pieces of cardboard or plastic place mats. That way, you can easily remove them when you need the work surface, and then can put them back when you've finished. This also prevents getting any sticky residue on your counters.

Cats generally don't like citrus scents, so you might try a bunch of lemon or orange peels—just stay away from essential oils, which can be toxic to cats. A sheet of aluminum foil may work, but some cats get used to the crinkly noise and the slippery feel, so the foil may lose its effectiveness over time.

Another possible remedy is the Snappy Trainer, which uses a mousetrap under a large, flat "paddle." When your cat walks across the paddle, the trap snaps, making a loud noise and flipping the paddle. It doesn't hurt your cat, but it sure can startle him.

Several cat owners swear by the Ssscat motion-activated deterrent, which warns your cat with noise when he trespasses. If the cat doesn't then move away from the forbidden surface, there's a blast of odorless, harmless gas. The canisters are battery operated, and you can move them around to different areas that you want to protect. Eventually, your cat should learn to avoid any area where he sees the canister.

While all of these methods will generally keep your cat off the kitchen counter, at least part of the time, you should make sure your cat has an alternate place to be, such as a shelf, a cat tree, or a sturdy bookcase that will not tip over. Leave the occasional tasty treat in your cat's special spot. Rotate special toys that your cat will only find in "his" place. Make it worth his while to spend time there, and not on the kitchen counter.

Partners in crime!

Cats can be taught appropriate scratching in kittenhood.

ats scratch. They scratch to mark their territory, to place their scent on objects, and to express themselves. Typically, a cat will stretch as high as he can while scratching, leaving a visible sign of his size. Cats also scratch to wear off the sheaths on their growing nails. Because scratching is instinctive, you're not going to be able to stop your cat from scratching. What you can do is redirect that scratching so that your cat is scratching acceptable items instead of your furniture and drapes.

Teaching your cat to use a scratching post is easier if you're starting with a kitten, and it's also easier if you start right away. Don't wait until your cat has already started to claw the arm of your sofa before you decide to invest in a scratching post. Get the post before you get the cat.

With a kitten or an adult, the first step is to get your cat's scent on the post. This will help mark the post as his, and he'll be more likely to return to it. Lure your cat to the post with a toy. As you twirl and wave the toy near the post, your cat will reach for the toy, putting his paws on the post. This may take a few tries, but eventually your cat will get the idea that the post is where he should scratch.

Vertical posts should be at least three feet high so your cat can stretch to his full length while scratching. Make sure that the post is sturdy and with a wide enough base so that your cat's weight won't tip it over. Once a cat has been frightened, or hurt, by a falling scratching post, it will be very hard to ever get him to use it again.

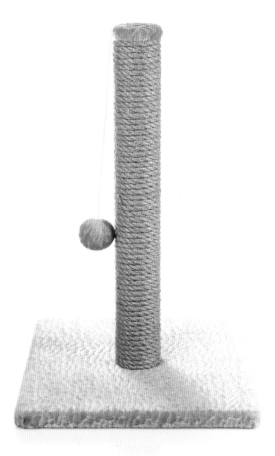

Choose a sturdy vertical post.

Most posts are wrapped in sisal, which is durable and can withstand the clawing action. Some posts may be covered in carpeting, but you won't want your cat to mistake your carpeting for his, so sisal may be the better choice.

While your cat is more likely to use a vertical scratching surface, there are also horizontal scratching pads, generally made of cardboard. To encourage use of a horizontal scratching pad, lightly dust it with catnip.

If you got your cat before you got a scratching post, and he's already in the habit of using your furniture to sharpen his claws, there are some techniques you can use to correct that behavior. First, cover the areas where your cat has been scratching with double-sided tape or sticky furniture strips made for this purpose (e.g., Sticky Paws). This will help prevent further damage because cats don't like the feel of sticky tape. If your cat has enjoyed climbing your drapes, hang the drapes on lightweight tension rods that will release from the wall when your cat's weight is added to the weight of the drapes.

Next, get your vertical and horizontal scratching posts and place them near the furniture that your cat has been scratching. Use a toy and catnip to encourage your cat to use the posts. Once your cat is using the proper posts for scratching, you can start to move them to more appropriate locations.

Don't rush this process! Move the post just a few inches each time. Leave it in the new location for two or three days before the next small move. If you move it too far away too quickly, your cat will just revert to scratching the furniture.

Another solution you can try while you're waiting for your cat to fully use a scratching post is to place soft covers on your cat's nails. These are made of vinyl or rubber and come in assorted colors as well as clear. They don't hurt the cat, and they can stop him from damaging furniture or drapes while he's making the transition to a scratching post.

IT'S MINE!

If you decide to add another cat (or two!) to your family, you may need more than one scratching post. Cats can be territorial over their scratching posts and not let other cats use them.

Some cat toys include a scratching surface.

20 Midnight Zoomies

The midnight zoomies can hit anytime, but it's usually when you're asleep. You may be suddenly awoken by a zooming cat running right across your outstretched body, or—ouch!—your face, seemingly for no apparent reason.

Cats in the wild hunt at dawn and dusk, so around the time when you're winding down for the day, your cat is ready to be active. Plus, cats sleep most of the day, so it stands to reason that if they're going to be active, it's going to be later in the day. At that time, your cat is on high alert, watching for prey, and sometimes all of his pent-up energy needs an outlet. Maybe your cat is testing out his fighting maneuvers or hunting techniques. Whatever the reason, the zoomies generally happen after dark.

If your cat's zoomies are really disruptive to your sleep, close the bedroom door. You can also try playing with your cat just before bedtime. An exciting game chasing a fake bird or toy mouse will help your cat expend some of his excess energy. Then, top off the play session with a nice helping of canned food. The combination of exercise and a full stomach may help end the midnight zoomies. Otherwise, you'll just have to get used to it.

The zoomies can send a cat bounding all over the house.

Y ou may find your cat sucking on a blanket or sweater. He may also suck on a bathmat or rug, and some cats may suck on another cat's tail or on their own paws—it doesn't specifically have to be wool.

Siamese and related breeds are more prone than others to suck wool, but any cat weaned too early or removed from his mother and littermates too early may have this habit. Kittens should never be taken from their mothers before eight weeks, and twelve weeks is even better.

This behavior isn't dangerous to the cat unless he starts to actually eat the fabric. Ingesting the fabric could cause an intestinal blockage, not to mention holes in your sweater or blanket.

If your cat is sucking wool, remove the items he is sucking and put them out of reach. Give him a stuffed toy to see if it will work as a substitute. Otherwise, play with your cat and give him interactive toys to take his mind off the sucking. Sometimes adding fiber to the diet, such as mixing a bit of wheat or oat bran into his food, helps.

Watch your cat for any tendency toward wool sucking.

You could even offer him a small pot of grass to chew on. Your cat might even enjoy gnawing on a raw bone (no cooked ones, and no chicken bones). The good news is that he'll likely outgrow the wool sucking habit as he ages.

22 Spraying

praying should not be confused with regular urination. Unless there's a medical reason, or your cat dislikes his litter box or litter, he should be urinating in the litter box. Spraying is when your cat sprays urine on a vertical surface. If you find a puddle, he's urinating where he shouldn't, but if a door, window, or wall is wet, the cat is spraying.

Spraying can be a problem with any cat, but it can intensify in multiple-cat households. A cat sprays to mark his territory, so, the more cats, the more one or more of them may feel the need to mark "his" space to warn off another cat. A cat will also mark around doors and windows if he sees another

cat in his yard. It's the cat's way of telling the stranger to stay away. Cats may also spray if they are upset, and many things can cause them to become upset, from a new addition to the family (human or animal) to the furniture's being rearranged.

Sometimes the solution is as easy as shutting the blinds or drawing the drapes on a particular window. Sometimes it may take some detective work to determine what is causing the spraying. Spraying is hard to prevent, but you may find that diffusing a product with synthetic cat hormones may help by relaxing your cat while you work to discover what is triggering the spraying.

Keep a clean litter box to encourage your cat to use it.

Under normal circumstances, a cat should be using his litter box.

A cat may climb up a tree after a bird or squirrel, or he may go up in a tree to escape an enemy. Now what? He may settle down on a comfortable branch and meow pitifully. Don't panic. Cats climb up much more easily than they climb down. Going up, their claws are curved the right way to help them make the climb. Coming down, they need to go backward, and it's much harder.

Cats can climb up, but it's much harder for them to get down.

If a dog chased the cat, and the dog is still at the base of the tree, encourage him to go away. Then, ignore your cat for a while. If you're panicking, your cat will be afraid, too.

If you can't stand the inactivity, go to the store and buy some birdseed. If your cat is still in the tree, sprinkle the birdseed around the base of the tree. When birds arrive to eat the seed, the sight of those fluttering wings may encourage your cat to climb down. Or, you might just try calling your cat while you use a can opener to open a tasty can of tuna or cat food.

While it may take awhile, most cats will come down eventually. If you think for some reason that your cat is truly stuck, and you have a long enough ladder, you can try to rescue him, but be careful. Wear heavy gloves to protect your hands. Your normally loving cat may not appreciate being removed from his safe perch. Take along a cloth sack or a pillowcase so that you can carry the cat down without worrying about sharp teeth and slashing claws.

On the extremely rare occasions when a cat can't get down from a tree, and you've been waiting all day, or overnight, call your local animal control for suggestions. Many fire departments will no longer remove cats from trees, but maybe you could call a tree trimming service.

No matter the solution, try to remain calm. No one's ever found a cat skeleton in a tree.

PART IV

The Litter Box

The litter box is a "good news/bad news" item. The good news is that cats instinctively bury their waste, so your cat will use a litter box. You don't have to build your schedule around when you need to take the cat out, the way you do with dogs. You can stay out late, or even overnight, without worrying about your cat. The bad news is that you need to put a litter box somewhere that is easily accessible to your cat but at the same time discreetly hidden.

Your cat may not mind going down into the basement, or he may ignore that location completely. Even if he's fine with the basement, he may start to have difficulty negotiating the stairs multiple times a day as he ages.

Some people put the litter box in a storage closet, but if the smell builds up, your cat may ignore that location. If you have an enclosed porch, that might work, but if you live in a cold climate, your cat may decide it's too cold to use the box. Many people put the litter box in a bathroom. If you're lucky and have a rarely used powder room, that might be the best solution. One place never to put the litter box is next to your cat's food and water dishes. You wouldn't want to eat your meals in the bathroom, and neither do cats.

Once you've settled on a location, you need the litter box itself, and there are many choices. Some boxes are triangular so that they fit into a corner. Some have a lip on them to help contain the litter. You can buy a covered litter box that keeps the litter and odor from spreading and is a bit more attractive, but some cats just don't like covered boxes. While a covered box has the advantage of keeping things hidden, it also traps and holds odors. If your cat is turned off by the smell, he won't use the box. He might rather go behind the sofa than use the box. Since communication with cats isn't up to these kinds of specifics yet, you won't know until you try.

Your kitten won't know what to do with the litter box at first, but he will learn quickly.

Place your litter box where your cat can find it but where it will be out of the way.

There are also motorized litter boxes. One kind senses movement. There's a delay to make sure the cat is out of the box, and then a motor starts and a huge "comb" runs through the litter, dragging the waste into a closed cylinder for disposal. You use clumping litter with this kind of box so that all waste gets removed. These litter boxes are fairly expensive, but it assures a clean box all of the time. Of course, some cats don't like clumping litter, and, if a cat happens to be around when the motorized box is working, the noise may deter him from ever using that particular box again.

Another type of litter box works almost like a toilet. It dissolves all of the kitty waste with water that then runs through a hose that you hook up to either a drain or your toilet. A sprayer sprays the litter with a cleaning solution, and a dryer dries the litter. The litter used with this box is plastic granules, thus eliminating the problem of what to do with used litter—it just keeps getting recycled.

The major drawback to this type of unit is the cost, which can be hundreds of dollars, depending on whether you get a covered one, plus the monthly cost of refilling the cleaning fluid.

A second drawback is that it is a bit noisy, so cats might not like it. Again, if your cat doesn't like it, he won't use it. A few hundred dollars is a lot to spend, only to find out that your cat is a traditionalist and wants an old-fashioned litter box with no running water.

Speaking of water, a third drawback is that this litter box uses the equivalent of a flush and a half's worth of water every time it cleans itself. On the plus side, you set the schedule for the flushes, so you could have it flush just once or twice a day. Just make sure that it's being cleaned frequently enough that your cat continues to use it. If it gets too dirty, your cat will go elsewhere.

An alternative to the litter box is to teach your cat to use the human toilet. You already have at least one in your home, and I've been told that it's fairly easy to teach your cat to use the toilet. You can use a special training kit to help you. There's a plastic insert that fits the toilet seat, and you cover the insert with litter. You gradually lessen the amount of litter and, one day, remove the insert. The cat then perches on the edge of the seat and, when he's finished, you flush.

This sounds great, but unless you have more than one bathroom, you are going to have to remove this training unit every time a human member of the family needs to use the toilet. I'm not sure how long it takes to train a cat with this method, but it could result in a fair amount of spilled litter. And what about those middle-of-the-night visits (yours, not the cat's)? You know, when you stagger down the hall with your eyes closed, trying not to wake up all the way. That's just when I'd probably forget all about the litter on the toilet seat—until I sat down.

In spite of scooping, disposing of used litter, and regularly cleaning the litter pan, the old-fashioned litter box seems to have a lot in its favor, except for one thing: most commercial litter boxes are too small. Your best bet may be to buy a plastic storage bin and cut down one side to make entry into the box easy.

Once you have your litter box, you may decide that using a litter-box liner is just the thing. Instead of trying to empty the box and possibly spilling some of the contents, you can neatly dispose of everything by removing the liner and litter together. The problem is that many cats don't like the feel of a liner when they're digging. And, I'll repeat: what a cat doesn't like, he will avoid. If you try a liner, keep an eye on your cat for the first few days to see if he's using the box or if he's taken his business elsewhere.

The same goes for using mats to surround a litter box. These are meant to trap litter and prevent it from being tracked around the house, but those mats may offend sensitive paws, especially those of cats who have been declawed.

Litter may seem like a straightforward topic, but sometimes it seems as if there are as many types of litter as there are breeds of

NO LITTER?

While most cats do use some type of litter, occasionally there are cats who prefer no litter at all. Such a cat may use only an empty litter box or one with just a single layer of newspaper or paper towel on the bottom. If your cat has expressed disdain for all of the types of litter you've offered, try one of these options instead.

cat. You can get clay litter, deodorizing litter, or clumping litter. There are biodegradable litters made from alfalfa, corncob, citrus peels, and wheat. Some litters are "flushable" (most are not, so read the label carefully before you dispose of any litter).

Scented litter can seem like a great idea. The problem is that a scent that appeals to a human may not appeal to a cat. If the scented litter is offensive to a feline nose, that cat will find somewhere else to relieve himself. Texture can also be a problem. The ancestors of the domestic cat likely had soft, fine sand to use, so coarser litter may not agree with your cat. And, cats are individuals. What one cat loves, another may hate. So, don't stock up on a particular kind of litter until you're sure your cat will like it. Some people will set up three or more boxes with different litters to see which their cat prefers. If you're getting your cat from a breeder or a neighbor, ask what litter the cat has been using.

This all may sound complicated, but even if you need to experiment with a box or litter, it won't take long for your cat to fall into a routine of regular litter box use.

Multiple Cats

This book is intended to help you prepare for getting your first cat, but, frequently, people with one cat think that a second cat is a great idea. Sometimes that second cat leads to a third. So let's pretend that you've gone beyond one cat. The whole litter box dynamic is likely to change. For instance, your first cat might be fine with a covered litter box, but your second cat may hate it. Besides the buildup of odors, maybe one cat tends to pick on another cat. The bullied cat may not want to use a litter box where he can be trapped. The different cats may each prefer a different litter. Some cats who are otherwise friendly just don't want to share a litter box.

For these reasons, the rule of thumb is one litter box per cat, plus one extra. That doesn't mean putting them all in a row, either. If you have a multilevel house, you'll want at least one litter box on each floor. It's essential that every cat is comfortable using a litter box.

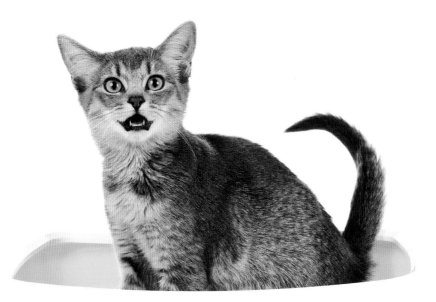

Cats are very clean animals, but even the cleanest cat is going to leave odors behind in the litter box. If your cat is spraying, that will leave an odor as well. Scoop the litter box at least once a day, or whenever you notice a "deposit." The cleaner you keep the box, the less likely your cat will go elsewhere.

Wash the box thoroughly at least once a week. If you are cleaning anything other than the litter box, never use ammonia as a cleaning agent. Urine contains ammonia, and the ammonia scent will encourage your cat to use that area as a bathroom. With a litter box, the ammonia smell won't matter because that's where your cat is supposed to go. Just remember to rinse thoroughly anyway because too strong a smell can drive your cat away.

A clean litter box keeps odors down and your cat happy.

You'll eventually need to replace plastic litter boxes because the odor will build up in the plastic. To add life to the litter box, clean it with a mild bleach-and-water solution. Fill the box and let it soak for at least twenty minutes. Rinse thoroughly and then wash with mild dish soap. Rinse and let air-dry.

If your cat has decided that some other area is a great place to either urinate or spray, here are some other suggestions. Use bleach, depending on the surface. You won't want to use bleach on upholstery or carpeting, and maybe not on certain other surfaces, either. Rubbing alcohol also works. It's relatively inexpensive and evaporates quickly. Test it before using it on textiles. A friend uses an enzymatic stain and odor cleaner (such as Nature's Miracle), which works well on everything except thick upholstery.

A product that is very good for getting rid of urine odor is Zero Odor. The company makes a product specifically for pet odors, and it also makes a product to add to laundry that will help make your pet's bedding smell fresh. Note: Zero Odor for laundry does have a floral scent.

No matter what product you use to clean up after your cat, remember that if your cat has always used a litter box but is now avoiding it and going elsewhere, there may be a medical reason. Any abnormal behavior in any pet is cause for concern. Schedule an appointment with your veterinarian. Caught early, many issues can be easily treated, but if you delay, you could endanger your pet's long-term health.

PART V:
Feeding Your Cat

Food and Your Cat 26

Food is made up of protein, carbohydrates, fat, vitamins, and minerals. Food, along with water, is what keeps life going.

Protein is made up of amino acids and is needed for growth and strong muscles. Carbohydrates supply energy and help with digestion. Fat also supplies energy, and it carries certain vitamins and can help a cat use those vitamins. Vitamins and minerals help cats process the other food eaten, they help with bone growth and vision, and they affect the way the nervous system functions. Minerals help with healthy blood flow and healing.

Mammals can produce some of the amino acids they need. When they can't produce an amino acid, but must get it from the food they eat, that amino acid is called an essential amino acid. For cats, a crucial essential amino acid is taurine. Lack of taurine can cause heart problems, blindness, and even death. Unlike other mammals, cats can't make enough taurine, and meat is the only thing that contains taurine. You can't get taurine from eating plants. That's why cats are called obligate carnivores. They must have meat to live.

There are also fatty acids that are essential to cats. While plants do synthesize fatty acids, relying on plant sources alone for fatty acids may lead to liver and kidney problems, as well as stunted muscle growth, in your cat.

Cats also use fewer fats and carbohydrates than other mammals. They don't have the ability to use carbohydrates the way dogs and people do, for instance. With that in mind, don't presume that cat and dog food are interchangeable. A cat living on dog food is a malnourished cat. The carbohydrates that a dog might effectively use are worthless calories to a cat. Cats need more protein as well as different quantities of vitamins and fatty acids. Kittens need one and a half times more protein than puppies, and adult cats need two to three times the amount of protein that adult dogs need.

The bottom line is that cats need the nutrients in meat to survive.

Cats lack the enzymes necessary to turn beta-carotene in plants to vitamin A, so they again must rely on meat to supply the vitamin A that is needed for maintaining vision, growth, and reproduction. Cats need five times the thiamine that dogs do. It's important to give your cat fresh food because the longer commercial food is stored, the less thiamine remains. Cats need vitamin D from their food because, unlike humans, they can't get it through their skin. They need animal fat and some liver (but not too much, as it can cause vitamin A toxicity).

Cats need the moisture provided by wet food.

While your cat may enjoy crunching on some dry food as a snack, it's not a good idea to rely solely on dry food. Cats need wet food to supply the water they need.

BENEFITS OF WATER

Regular *Huffington Post* contributor Donna Solomon, DVM, notes that "higher water intake equates to more dilute urine and lower incidence of crystal formation in urine. In addition, cats fed canned food have a lower incidence of hyperthyroidism, diabetes, constipation, and obesity."

Cats, being descendents of desert-dwelling felines, don't have the same reaction to thirst or dehydration that other animals do. If their food doesn't contain sufficient moisture, they are not as likely as other animals to find water. Cats who hunt get the moisture they need from their prey (mice, for instance, are about 70 percent water). Because your pet cat will not be hunting to survive, it's up to you to make sure you feed him in such a way that gives him that moisture he needs.

Whether you feed dry, wet, raw, home-cooked, or a combination of food types, keep in mind the very specific nutritional needs of a domestic cat.

Types of Food and How to Feed

No matter what you choose to feed your cat, the best times of day to feed may be early morning and early evening because those are the times when a wild cat would normally be hunting and eating in the wild. In fact, cats do better with several small meals rather than one large one, so you can offer canned food three or four times a day and leave out some dry food for the times when your cat wants a snack.

Cats need roughly two hundred calories a day, and it's not true that they won't ever eat too much. While a cat may not gulp food the way a dog would, a cat can eat too much and, without much exercise, can become obese. Also, the feeding amount recommended on packaged food may be excessive. It will be trial and error with your own cat, but watch your cat's weight and adjust his food portions accordingly. You should always be able to feel your cat's ribs. If you can see them, the cat is probably too thin, but if you can't feel them, it's diet time.

Cats enjoy their food at room temperature, so consider warming up leftover canned food that has been in the refrigerator. You can do this by putting the food in a plastic zipper-seal bag and placing the bag in a bowl of warm water for a few minutes prior to feeding. If you use a microwave, put the food in a microwave-safe bowl and make sure that you stir the food after heating so there are no hot spots.

No single food or type of food is right for all cats. Cats, like people, can be allergic to some foods. The best food in the world won't be good for your cat if it makes him itch or gives him diarrhea, so you may need to experiment if your cat doesn't do well on certain foods. And I'll say it again: cats need meat. They cannot live healthy lives without it. They have specific dietary needs that can be met only by meat.

Types of Cat Food

Commercial canned and dry cat foods offer convenience and a balanced diet. They are consistent in terms of percentages of ingredients and have been tested in food trials. They are relatively easy to store and are generally readily available. You typically find them in grocery stores and pet-supply shops.

There are some commercially available specialty foods that are also becoming popular. Most of these are raw foods in freeze-dried, fresh, and frozen forms. While some pet-supply stores carry these, many types must be ordered, and they are generally more expensive than canned and dry foods.

If you feed a quality commercial food, your cat will most likely do very well. Some people, though, prefer to cook for their cats. They like knowing where the food came from, and some may purchase only organic products for their cats. Home cooking does not mean just scraping leftovers into a bowl for your cat. You need to consider the proper

Canned foods contain the meat and water that cats need.

FREEZE-DRIED FOODS

You must mix freeze-dried foods with water to rehydrate them. Some must also be mixed with a protein in the form of cooked or raw meat. Freeze-dried foods have a long shelf life and are lightweight. Because they are freeze-dried, they contain no preservatives. Freeze-dried foods for cats are usually raw.

balance of protein, fat, fiber, vitamins, and minerals, which is different for cats than it is for humans.

Cats cannot digest certain human foods, and others may cause illness or even death in cats. Here are a few examples:

- **Cats don't need, and generally aren't able to use, vegetables.**

- **Cooked eggs are fine, but a protein in raw egg whites can interfere with the absorption of biotin, which is essential for the growth of cells, metabolism of fat, and transference of carbon dioxide.**

- **Onions can cause hemolytic anemia in cats.**

These are just a few examples of human foods that are not good for cats. You might not intentionally feed harmful foods to your cat, but you need to be careful that your cat can't reach these foods and that everyone in the family knows that these

foods are forbidden. You can read more on harmful human foods in the Sharing Your Food section (page 88).

If you decide to cook for your cat, check with a feline nutritionist to make sure that the meals are balanced for your cat. You can then cook up a large batch of food and freeze it in meal-sized portions. If you board your cat, make sure that the kennel can store your cat's food in a refrigerator or freezer. If you travel with your cat, you'll have to bring a cooler to store and transport your cat's food.

Many people feel that the best way to feed a cat is to give raw food. You may hear raw feeding referred to as the BARF (Bones And Raw Food/Biologically Appropriate Raw Food) diet or the Frankenprey diet. Be warned that no one seems to be neutral on the topic of raw diets. People who feed raw boast of their cats' shiny coats, white teeth, and overall good health. Opponents warn of bacterial contamination and the risk of parasite infestation and toxin ingestion.

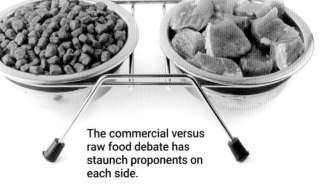

The commercial versus raw food debate has staunch proponents on each side.

Some veterinarians are in favor of raw feeding, and some are against it. If you find a terrific veterinarian who has reservations about raw diets, and you want to try it with your cat, ask what tests she might want to run on a regular schedule to make sure your cat is healthy and thriving on the raw food.

Feeding raw does not mean just throwing down a chunk of meat, either. Once again, you need to be aware of the proper balance. Most people who feed raw combine raw meaty bones with organ meat.

Bones are an important part of feeding raw, but the bones must be both fresh and raw. Recreational chewing is fine, but after two or three days, a raw bone dries out and can be just as dangerous as a cooked bone. To avoid potential problems, some people grind all bones before giving them to their cats.

If you do decide to feed raw, you should know that cats and dogs fed raw have a higher percentage of *Salmonella* (30 percent as opposed to 10 percent) in their system than animals fed cooked food, but they can tolerate this. It's people who are more likely to be affected by *Salmonella* in preparing raw foods. If you feed raw, wash your hands frequently and disinfect food-preparation surfaces. Also, because 10 percent of *Salmonella* on dishes can survive being rinsed with bleach and being washed in the dishwasher, use disposable dishes when feeding raw. You can use inexpensive paper plates, and your cat won't mind in the least.

GROUND MEAT

One source (*www.catsndogs naturally.com*) states that grinding meat dissipates the taurine content, giving your cat less taurine than it should. One thing is definite: when any meat is ground, the surface bacteria is spread throughout the meat, allowing bacteria to grow at a more rapid rate. Use extra care when handling ground raw-meat products.

Reading Food Labels

If your choice is a commercial food, the first thing you need to do is learn how to read the label. The Association of American Feed Control Officials (AAFCO) certifies all commercial cat foods. This means that a food meets certain standards and is appropriate for the cat. The label may also state whether the food is intended for all ages, for kittens, for geriatric cats, or for cats with specific needs. Here are some definitions to help you decipher cat-food labels.

BUYING RAW

You'll find multiple companies that offer raw food in convenient packaging. Some offer whole animals, such as rabbits and mice, and some offer traditional meats cut into portions. Some may offer ground meats, which may also contain ground bones.

MEAT: Meat refers to animal muscle tissue and will not include bone, but it may include fat and gristle. The type of meat should be designated. However, if the label just says "meat," it must be from cattle, pigs, sheep, or goats. If the meat is from another source, then it must specify the source, and it may be something like rabbit or bison. The definition of meat does not include poultry or fish.

MEAT BY-PRODUCTS: These are other clean parts of the animal, such as the lungs, spleen, kidneys, brain, or liver. Meat by-products can't include hair, horns, teeth, or hooves. While meat by-products may not sound very appealing to us, they can provide nutrition for your cat.

POULTRY: Poultry can be any kind of poultry and, unless specified, will include both flesh and bone. Bone is a good source of calcium, so don't be put off by its inclusion. Poultry can't include feathers, heads, feet, or entrails.

POULTRY BY-PRODUCTS: Poultry by-products may include hearts, gizzards, livers, and other internal organs, as well as heads and feet. Again, try to look at the by-products for their nutritional value.

Another good reason to check the ingredient list is because product names can be misleading if you don't understand them. For instance, if a label says "chicken cat food," then it must contain 95 percent of whatever ingredient is named, not including moisture content. If the product name mentions two ingredients, such as "chicken and tuna cat food," then there has to be

Read the labels on commercial cat foods so you can make healthy choices.

Chicken is a popular protein source in cat food.

more chicken than tuna, but the total needs to be 95 percent, so it could be 48 percent chicken and 47 percent tuna or 90 percent chicken and 5 percent tuna.

If a food contains less than 95 percent but more than 25 percent meat or fish, the name must have a qualifier, such as "dinner," "entrée," or "formula." Here's where you need to check the list of ingredients, because a "chicken dinner" might contain more fish than chicken, and if your cat were allergic to fish, this could be a disaster. If more than one ingredient is included in a "dinner," then the combination of the two must equal 25 percent, with each named ingredient accounting for at least 3 percent.

If the word "with" is in the food's name, it needs to include only 3 percent of the named ingredient—so "chicken cat food" will contain 95 percent chicken, whereas "cat food with chicken" may contain only 3 percent chicken.

As if all of this isn't confusing enough, the Food and Drug Administration (FDA) says that "premium" and "ultra-premium" foods are not required to be better, or healthier, than any other complete and balanced cat food. What's more, there are no official definitions for "natural" or "organic." Some manufacturers use "natural" to mean that there are no artificial or added preservatives. Most cat foods have vitamins and minerals added, and those are usually man-made, so "all-natural" may be misleading. A label could say "natural with added vitamins and minerals."

Speaking of preservatives, they are essential in dry foods to prevent the fats in them from spoiling. If the food company chooses a natural preservative, the food will not last as long as a food preserved with a synthetic preservative. Natural preservatives include vitamin E (mixed tocopherols), vitamin C (ascorbic acid), and extracts of various plants, such as rosemary. Common man-made preservatives are BHT (butylated ydroxytoluene) and BHA (butylated hydroxyanisole).

If you prefer natural preservatives, remember that a preservative only needs to be listed if the manufacturer has added it. The manufacturer may use a meat source that adds artificial preservatives to the meat, and that will not show up on the label. If you want absolutely no preservatives of any kind, stick with canned food only.

According to the FDA, many states require pet food to guarantee the minimum

PROTEIN QUALITY

According to the PetCoach website (*www.petcoach.co*), some proteins are better than others, and "the ability of a protein to be used by the body . . . is summarized as protein quality." Comparing protein sources to determine their quality is helpful whether you are reading nutrition labels or cooking for your cat. The website lists the following biological values for certain common proteins, with a higher number indicating a higher-quality protein: egg, 100; fishmeal and milk, 92; beef, approximately 78; and soybean meal, 67. With cats, steer away from plant proteins and offer your pet the animal proteins that his body can most effectively use.

percentages of crude protein and crude fat and the maximum percentages of crude fiber and moisture. Some manufacturers include other guarantees as well. What you need to know when comparing nutritional values of dry and canned food is how to convert guarantees to a moisture-free basis. Here's the formula presented by the FDA:

- **Find the percentage of whatever you want to measure and find the moisture percentage.**

- **Subtract the moisture percentage from 100 to get the dry-weight percentage.**

- **Divide the protein (or whatever) percentage by the dry-weight percentage and multiply that number by 100. That total is the dry-weight percentage.**

Usually, the dry matter in dry food is about four times the amount in canned food. Canned food usually has more protein while kibble contains more fiber.

DID YOU KNOW?

Cats don't need vegetables, and some can even be harmful.

28 Sharing Your Food

Many people enjoy sharing safe treats with their cats occasionally.

It's always fun to share a snack or offer a special treat to your cat. Cats aren't as likely to beg for a potato chip or piece of cheese as dogs are, but there are still human foods they might enjoy. Cats have a reputation for being finicky eaters, but many cats enjoy cantaloupe and corn on the cob; cat-owning friends have also cited broccoli, asparagus, green beans, brussels sprouts, and tomato sauce. Some cats will nibble cream cheese and ice cream, and one friend even has a cat who likes nacho cheese tortilla chips.

Most of the time, though, the treat your cat will prefer is meat, and it's good for him. All meat contains taurine, which is essential for your cat's good health. So, a bite of meat makes a tasty, healthy snack. Dark poultry meat is also an excellent source of taurine.

Your cat might enjoy chewing shreds of meat off a bone, but be careful. A raw bone is fine, but a cooked bone can shatter and, if your cat swallows a shard, it could pierce his stomach or intestine. If you do offer your cat a raw bone, remember it will become as dry as a cooked bone after about three days, so you will need to take it away.

Chances are, your cat will come running when you open a can of tuna, but don't overdo that fishy treat. Too much tuna can lead to mercury poisoning. Cats are much smaller than people, so it will take far less tuna to poison a cat. If a cat eats large amounts of tuna, he can develop steatitis, a condition characterized by lumps under the skin accompanied by fever and abdominal pain.

Tuna is a favorite of most every cat but should only be offered in limited amounts.

Watch your cat's intake of other fish, too. While a bit of fish makes a nice treat, many cats are allergic to fish, even though most cats love it. Also, according to Jean Hofve, DVM, the fish in many cat foods is ground up, bones and all, and "excess phosphorus is dangerous for kitties with kidney disfunction; there is as much phosphorus as calcium in bones."

Also, according to the Cat Health website, *www.cathealth.com*, fish is high in magnesium, which can lead to the formation of struvite crystals in a cat's urine, which in turn can cause a urinary tract disease and urethral blockage in male cats. Fish also contains a high amount of iodine, and that may increase a cat's risk of developing hyperthyroidism.

Offer any raw meat or fish with caution, as there is a danger of *Salmonella*, and, with raw fish, there's another danger as well. An enzyme in raw fish destroys thiamine, which is an essential vitamin for your cat. A lack of thiamine can lead to convulsions and may put your cat into a coma.

The bottom line is that you should limit the fish you feed your cat and check the ingredients in your cat food. Fish may sound like a good ingredient, but it can cause problems.

Cooked liver makes a great training aid, but keep liver in the treat category rather than in the dinner category. Too much liver can cause vitamin A toxicity, which can affect bone growth or even cause death.

We're all familiar with the image of a cat happily lapping up a saucer of milk, but the truth is that most adult cats are lactose intolerant. Too much of any dairy product can lead to digestive upset, complete with diarrhea. That teaspoon of milk at the bottom of your cereal bowl is probably fine, but stay away from too much milk.

A little milk is fine from time to time, but too much dairy is not good for cats.

Maybe your cat likes to share your scrambled eggs with you in the morning. That's another safe treat, but stay away from raw eggs. There's a protein in raw egg whites that can interfere with your cat's absorption of biotin. No need to panic if you drop an egg and your cat laps up a bit, but don't make raw eggs a part of your cat's diet.

So far, all of the foods mentioned are safe for your cat, even if in limited amounts, but the following foods are definite no-nos. The good news is that cats, unlike dogs, don't have much of a sweet tooth. The odds are good that your cat won't devour that chocolate bar or gobble down a box of raisins. Still, it's good to know what foods are harmful, just in case.

ONIONS: Whether cooked, raw, or powdered, onions can break down red blood cells, leading to anemia. A large amount all at once, or a small amount regularly, can cause trouble. Keep your cat away from garlic and chives, too, to prevent gastrointestinal upset.

GRAPES AND RAISINS: Never offer a raisin or a grape as a treat, because they can cause severe kidney damage. Even a small amount can lead to vomiting and hyperactivity.

CHOCOLATE: It's hard to believe that something as delicious as chocolate can be deadly, but, for our feline friends, that's the case. Chocolate contains theobromine, a chemical that can be lethal to a cat. The darker the chocolate, the higher the concentration of theobromine. Chocolate can cause abnormal heart rhythms, seizures, and death. Keep chocolate out of reach and never share any with your cat.

COFFEE: You might think it's cute if your cat tries to get a taste of your morning coffee or your afternoon soft drink, but caffeine, which gives humans a nice boost, can be

Your cat will enjoy a treat of scrambled eggs, but never give him raw eggs.

Caffeine isn't good for any animals, cats included.

fatal for your cat. Depending on the amount ingested, caffeine can cause restlessness, rapid breathing, heart palpitations, and muscle tremors. Larger amounts can even cause death. Besides beverages, caffeine is in some cold medicines and painkillers, another reason to never use medicine meant for humans on your cat.

ALCOHOL: Alcoholic beverages should also be kept away from your cat. A drunken animal is never funny, and any amount of alcohol is too much for a cat. Just two teaspoons of whiskey can send your cat into a coma, and a third teaspoon could kill him.

XYLITOL: Xylitol is an artificial sweetener sometimes used in diet foods. Gum, candy, and toothpaste may also contain xylitol. This sugar substitute is fine for humans, but it can increase insulin levels in cats, which,

in turn, can cause blood sugar levels to drop. Symptoms of xylitol poisoning include vomiting, lethargy, loss of coordination, and seizures. Too much xylitol can lead to liver failure within days. As with other sweet products, your cat probably won't even be interested, but all cats are individuals, so play it safe and keep products containing xylitol away from your cat.

YEAST: Yeast dough is another hazard to cats. In the warmth of a cat's stomach, yeast dough can continue to rise, leading to discomfort, and, if he has eaten enough dough, to death.

It's okay to share the occasional healthy snack, like a bit of lean turkey, with your cat, but when in doubt, stick with treats made especially for cats. It's always best to err on the side of caution.

29 Food and Water Bowls

There are all kinds of food and water dishes on the market, and many are decorated with adorable kitty designs, but look beyond the artwork. Your three basic choices are plastic, ceramic, and stainless steel.

Plastic dishes are probably the cheapest. They are lightweight and don't easily break. They come in many colors, and most are dishwasher safe. Plastic, however, can invite chewing, and scratches in the plastic made by teeth can harbor harmful bacteria. Also, if the cat's chin constantly rubs on the plastic, it can lead to a case of feline acne.

If a plastic dish is not dishwasher-safe, it can be very hard to thoroughly clean, leading to staining and possible odor. If you have decided to feed raw, definitely cross plastic off your list of dish choices. In fact, if you are feeding raw, stick to nonporous stainless steel or disposable paper. Plastic bowls may be the cheapest, but they are not the best.

Ceramic dishes are heavy and can't easily be shoved around the room the way plastic can. Ceramic can break, though, and if you choose ceramic bowls, make sure that the paint or glaze is lead-free.

Stainless steel is almost indestructible. It is lightweight, easy to clean, and nonporous. It comes in a wide variety of shapes and sizes, and many stainless-steel bowls have rubber rings on the bottom to help keep them in one spot.

You may discover that your cat is happiest eating from a saucer or small plate from your

Ceramic bowls are easy to clean but breakable.

Stainless-steel bowls are the all-around best choices for food and water bowls.

own cupboard. That's because a plate or saucer gives a cat's whiskers plenty of room, and they will not bend. Your own dishes should be lead-free and dishwasher-safe.

Domestic cats evolved from desert ancestors, so cats don't tend to drink as much water as dogs do. They get much of their needed water content from their food. According to Dr. Mark E. Peterson on the blog for his veterinary practice, the Animal Endocrine Clinic in New York, cats in the wild get most of their water from freshly killed prey, which contains about 70 to 75 percent water, depending on what is caught.

Feeding wet food is a good way to help make sure that your cat gets the water he needs because most canned food contains 67 to 73 percent water. It's not a good idea to feed dry food exclusively, because cats just don't drink as much as many other animals. Dr. Peterson further notes that domestic

cats have a diminished "thirst drive." When they are dehydrated, they are slower to drink enough to replenish the water in their systems. Dogs will replenish in one hour, but it can take a cat twenty-four hours to drink enough water.

Many cats prefer running water, and there are special fountains that keep fresh, clean water circulating for your cat's drinking pleasure. Your cat may prefer sipping directly from the faucet. Run a thin stream of water and see if your cat enjoys it. Some cats like to drink from a full glass of water. Maybe you'll need to keep a glass of water in the sink so that, if you allow your cat on the counter, he can help himself. Or you may need to place small containers of water in several locations. Cats can be picky about exactly where they'll drink.

Many people seem to think that their cats' dishes don't need to be washed. If the

Running water may encourage a cat to drink.

cat has licked the bowl clean, it's OK, right? But think about it. If you licked your dinner plate clean, would you put it back in the cupboard? A licked bowl is not a clean bowl. Wash your cat's food bowl after every meal, and wash his water bowl daily. If the bowls are dishwasher-safe, just pop them in with your dishes.

If you've decided to free-feed dry food, meaning that you will leave a bowl of kibble out for your cat all day, empty the dish at least once a day and clean it. If you're feeding wet food, don't let uneaten food sit in the bowl, breeding bacteria. Throw away uneaten food and clean the dish. Your cat doesn't ask for much. Give him a clean bowl.

Now, where are you going to put that food dish and water bowl? One place not to put either is anywhere near the litter box. Cats do not want to eat and drink where they eliminate. Putting his bowls in close proximity to the litter box may mean that your cat finds another location for elimination that's more desirable to him, but less desirable for you, or that he'll go on a hunger strike. Let's face it: if you were served your meals in the bathroom, you might start to avoid that room, too.

The kitchen is an obvious location for feeding, and an out-of-the-way corner is fine if your cat will be an only cat, with no competition for food. Because most cats like to be up high,

you can feed your cat on the kitchen counter if you allow him up there. Most people don't encourage their cats to be on food-preparation surfaces, but if you don't mind, your cat will be overjoyed.

If the top of your refrigerator is accessible, you could put your cat's food there as long as he can get up and down in easy stages.

You need to have a chair, stool, or some shelves available. No cat should be asked to climb or jump down from anything that high without some intermediate steps.

No matter the location that works for both you and your cat, remember to let him eat in peace.

Choose a place for your cat's bowls where he can eat without being disturbed.

PART VI:
Grooming Your Cat

Whether you have a short-coated cat who requires very little grooming or a Persian or Angora who needs attention daily, you'll need some basic grooming supplies. Yes, cats groom themselves, but there's only so much a tongue and a small paw can do.

No matter what kind of cat you have, have a supply of old towels handy. Towels are useful in all kinds of ways, from covering furniture to sopping up water if you have a cat like a Maine Coon or Turkish Van who thinks that the water bowl is a pool. If you plan to bathe your cat, you'll need more towels than you think.

Most cats will rarely, if ever, need a bath. Some hairless breeds may need occasional bathing to rid the skin of oils and dirt, and your cat may need a bath if he gets into something especially sticky or stinky. Otherwise, brushing or combing your cat (again, depending on coat type) may be all your cat ever needs.

In the unlikely event that you do need to bathe your cat, your kitchen sink or a stationary laundry tub will work just fine. If, for some reason, you'd rather use your bathtub, get a small pillow for your knees. Put a rubber mat in the bottom of the sink or tub so that your cat won't slip. If you're using the bathtub, and you have a handheld shower attachment, you can use that for washing your cat. Otherwise, you can buy a special attachment at a pet-supply store for the faucet in either the tub or your sink. Many kitchen sinks have sprayers, which work very well. If you don't have a sprayer and don't want to buy a special attachment, you can just use water from the tap and a pan or cup to wet and rinse your cat, but that takes much longer and makes it harder to get all of the soap out of your cat's coat.

Longhaired cats need more attention than those with short coats, but every cat needs some regular grooming.

Bath time will never be a favorite for many cats.

Towel-dry your cat gently to not create any tangles in his coat.

Some cats may enjoy a bath; others may sulk but hold relatively still. Still others will fight the very idea of a bath. One option is to put a small window screen at the end of the sink or tub so your cat can hold on with his claws, instead of sinking his claws into you.

To help contain your cat, use a small plastic bin or clothes basket. A clothes basket will let the water in but help keep your cat in one spot. Still, put a rubber mat in the bottom to keep your cat from slipping.

If you have a longhaired cat, give him a thorough brushing before wetting his coat because water will just worsen any mats and tangles. The water should be lukewarm, and you should adjust the water temperature before you put the cat in the water. You don't want to accidentally scald his feet while you're searching for the right temperature.

Always use a shampoo especially formulated for cats. Human shampoo will tend to dry out your cat's coat and skin. Wet your cat thoroughly, starting at the neck and working back. Try not to get water in your cat's ears. You can try to put a cotton ball in each ear, but your cat will likely just shake his head until the cotton comes out. Use a wet washcloth to wipe off your cat's muzzle and head.

Lather up the shampoo and squeeze it through your cat's coat, avoiding the head. Don't scrub because that will just tangle the coat. Rinse and repeat. Be sure to rinse thoroughly, paying special attention to the feet and to behind the elbows. Once you've finished rinsing, if you're lucky, your cat will shake while he's still in the tub. Otherwise, quickly wrap him in a towel and try to soak up as much water as you can before he shakes.

Lift or help him from the tub or sink. Don't let him scramble out on his own because he may injure himself.

If you're bathing your cat in the summer, you can just let your cat air-dry. If it's cold out, or if you have a cat with a very heavy coat, you'll need to use a hair dryer. If you use a hair dryer for humans, always use it on the lowest setting and always keep it moving over the cat. A human hair dryer, when on a higher setting, can burn your cat.

While you may not ever bathe your cat, even smooth-coated cats benefit from a good brushing. For short-coated cats, consider a pet grooming glove. This is a glove covered with little round nubs that help get rid of loose hair and dandruff. During shedding season, you can use a small, rubber brush

TEAR STAINS

Many breeds with shorter noses or with white or light-colored fur may get tear stains, which are rusty streaks on the face. A bit of hydrogen peroxide wiped on with a cotton swab can help diminish the stains.

with similar nubs to help remove dead hair. Finish by brushing your cat with a soft-bristle brush. Pet-supply stores sell nice boar's-bristle brushes, or you can use a human baby brush. A baby brush is also good for brushing off a cat's feet, which tend to be more sensitive that the rest of the body.

For cats with long fur, the brush with rubber nubs is good for removing dead guard hairs. Use long strokes, brushing in the direction of the fur. If your cat is shedding and has a thick undercoat, you'll want a special brush for shedding that grabs the loose undercoat. Use a comb to quickly run through the coat and to work on small tangles.

If you use a comb or a brush with metal teeth, be gentle. You don't want to scrape your cat's delicate skin. Spraying the coat with a light mist of water avoids breaking the individual hairs and helps control static electricity.

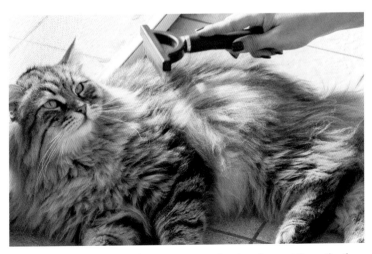

Special brushes and combs can remove dead undercoat from the fur.

31 Nail Clipping

You may think that if you supply your cat with a scratching post, and maybe a cat tree to play on, that those objects will keep your cat's nails trimmed, but you may still need to give your cat's nails a little help. A wild cat or a cat that lives completely outdoors may wear down the tips of his nails, but a house cat will probably still have very sharp tips in spite of regularly using the scratching post. Cutting off those sharp tips will prevent your cat from snagging a nail on carpeting and possibly breaking the nail. A broken nail can be painful and may get infected. Trimming your cat's nails will also make things more comfortable for you if your cat likes to curl up in your lap and knead your thighs.

Nail cutting is painless, but your cat may not like having his feet handled. Starting when a kitten is young is your best option, but even an adult cat can learn to relax and let you clip his nails. You just need to be patient.

BE CAREFUL OF THE QUICK

When you cut your cat's nails, try to avoid the quick, the dark blood vessel running through the middle of the nail. If you can't see the quick, cut the nail just where it starts to curve, and you should miss the quick. If you accidentally cut the quick, use a touch of styptic powder to stop the bleeding or just hold your finger tightly to the end of the nail until the bleeding stops.

First, just gently hold a paw so that your cat gets used to having his feet touched. Practice with all four paws. When your cat is comfortable with you holding his feet, gently take a paw in your hand and squeeze at the base of a toe to extend the claw. Don't try cutting the nail just yet. Just hold the clipper and let your cat smell it and get used to it. Give him a treat. Get him used to the noise of the clipper as well. Some people recommend snipping a piece of uncooked spaghetti, which will approximate the sound of the clipper cutting the nail.

When your cat is comfortable with both being handled and the presence of the clipper, clip a nail or two. Treat and praise your cat and release. Eventually, you'll work your way up to cutting all the nails. In the meantime, just be happy if you can do one paw at a time. Trim your cat's nails about every two weeks.

Regularly clipping the tips of your cat's nails benefits both of you.

There are different tools for cutting nails, and it's a matter of personal preference. A grinder is an electric or battery-powered tool with a rapidly rotating abrasive head that wears down the nail. The grinder is probably overkill with a cat because a cat's nails are much easier to snip than a dog's thicker nails. If you decide to use a grinding wheel to trim your cat's nails, don't just hold the wheel against the nail; move it around the nail and stop at intervals to let the heat dissipate.

If you have a set of sharp nail clippers for people, they will likely do the job, or you can buy special nail clippers for cats. If you buy

If nail trimming proves too much of a challenge, you can have it done at the vet's office.

Start by holding one paw and then press gently to extend the claws.

special nail scissors, make sure the blades are always sharp. There is also a guillotine-type trimmer with a sharp blade that slices through the nail. The advantage to this type of trimmer is that you can replace the blade when it gets dull rather than buying a new trimmer.

If you find that you really don't like clipping your cat's nails, or that your cat dislikes it so much that it's a chore for both of you, find a local groomer and let her do it. Whatever method you choose, just make sure that your cat's nails are trimmed regularly.

32 Deskunking Your Cat

I t's a fact that indoor cats live much longer than outdoor cats, but it's also a fact that many people choose to have cats who live both indoors and outdoors. If that's going to be your choice, you might someday need advice on how to treat a cat who's been sprayed by a skunk or gotten into some other undesirable substance. There's not much worse than the smell of skunk, unless it's the smell of skunk on your cat, who has just run past you into the house and who may be trying to get rid of the smell by rolling on the carpet or rubbing against the furniture.

The old remedy for deskunking used to be tomato juice, but it's messy and isn't always very effective. Plus, you need a lot of it, and not many of us keep a large stock of tomato juice in the pantry. Vinegar can work, and it's much less messy, but there's something that neutralizes the odor even better: a mixture of hydrogen peroxide, baking soda, and dishwashing liquid. Two of the ingredients you probably already have available all the time, and the other won't take up much room should you decide to stock a few bottles.

Any cat allowed outdoors risks an encounter with a stinky foe.

Mix sixteen ounces of hydrogen peroxide with two tablespoons of baking soda and one teaspoon of dishwashing liquid. You may need to wash your cat more than once, but this mixture will eliminate the odor. Mix it only when you're ready to use it.

Once you've cleaned up your cat, it's time to consider the furniture and carpeting that may have also picked up "eau de skunk" before you could catch your cat.

A product called Anti-Icky-Poo earns impressive reviews for removing skunk odor from carpets and upholstery. This product is not for your cat but for carpets, drapes, and furniture. If you don't have this product on hand, you can use one of the many oxygen-based cleaners on the market, or you can try the same hydrogen peroxide mixture that you used on your cat.

If your cat gets something sticky, such as tree sap, road tar, or even gum, in his coat, simply apply peanut butter or vegetable oil and use your fingers to rub the substance out. Ice cubes can also work; just remember not to let the ice rest on your cat's skin.

Hairspray and nail polish remover can also work. With hairspray, saturate the area, being careful not to get the spray in your cat's eyes. With nail polish remover, don't apply it directly, but soak a cotton ball or a rag in the remover and then apply it to the sticky substance. With both hair spray and polish remover, wash the area thoroughly afterward so that it doesn't irritate your cat's skin.

A dishwashing-liquid mixture can help "deskunk" your cat.

OWNER CLEANUP

If your cat rubbed some of the stink onto you, you can rid your clothes of the smell by using regular laundry detergent mixed with a half-cup of baking soda.

PART VII

ABCs of Healthcare

Just like people, cats can have allergies, and, just like with people, these allergies can develop anytime and may include dust, mildew, trees, grass, pollen, and mold. Your cat could also be allergic to a food or to flea bites. He may have a reaction to a drug or to a flea-control product. He may be allergic to perfume, certain cleaning products, or rubber or plastic. Whether he is technically allergic to cigarette smoke or not, getting a cat is another good reason to give up smoking. Secondhand smoke is as bad for cats as it is for humans.

Cats with allergies may have symptoms similar to those a human might show, including sneezing, coughing, and itchy or runny eyes. An inflamed throat may cause a cat to snore. A cat may have itchy skin, while an itchy back or itching at the base of the tail may indicate a flea allergy. If your cat is scratching his neck and head, that may mean a food allergy. Food allergies can also cause vomiting and/or diarrhea.

If your veterinarian suspects a food allergy, she'll probably recommend a special diet. Diets for allergic pets generally contain just one protein source, preferably one that your cat has never had before, like duck or venison. For twelve weeks, your cat will eat only that food, with no special treats or bites of human food. At the end of that time, you will slowly add other ingredients, one at a time, to try to determine what food is the cause of the problem. Alternatively, if you suspect a food allergy, you can switch to another brand of food or a formula with a different protein. Food allergies are notoriously hard to pin down.

Your veterinarian may recommend that you cook for your cat, but this is a very precise process, and it will take a long time to determine the allergen. If you decide on your own to cook for your cat, consult your veterinarian to make sure that you are offering a balanced diet with the required vitamins and minerals.

If your cat is allergic to fleas, only a few bites can lead to intense itching for two to three weeks.

Allergies can become itchy problems for affected cats.

A food-allergy diagnosis can mean strict dietary changes.

he may need an antihistamine shot before the swelling interferes with his breathing.

Besides causing itching, allergic reactions can cause asthma attacks. Your veterinarian may prescribe medications to open up your cat's breathing passages as well as corticosteroids for the long term.

Bathing your cat a couple of times a week will wash away pollens and other airborne irritants and may relieve itching. Talk to your veterinarian about a mild shampoo that won't dry out your cat's skin with frequent bathing. Shampoos containing oatmeal and aloe may be especially soothing. Also ask about giving your cat fatty acid supplements, which may also help with irritated skin.

A cat can catch fleas outdoors or from another pet.

Even if he's not allergic, fleas spread disease, so you'll want to eliminate them. Talk to your veterinarian about a flea-protection product. Even if your cat is an indoor cat, if you've got a dog that goes in and out, your cat can get fleas. A bath can get rid of the immediate problem, but then you should start using a flea preventative.

In some cases, such as with an ear infection or an insect sting, you'll need to treat the symptoms first. If something stings or bites your cat, and his face begins to swell,

Occasionally, an allergy may cause a cat to bite and lick his paws until a sore develops. These sores are called *lick granulomas* or *lick dermatitis*. While an allergy may be the underlying cause, the granuloma itself is likely to itch or hurt, causing the cat to lick and nibble even more, increasing the severity of the lick granuloma.

Ideally, you should treat the cause of the granuloma, if it can be determined. If the granuloma is severe, the cat may need a course of antibiotics. Meanwhile, you need to prevent the cat from continually licking that spot. He may need to wear an Elizabethan collar (or "cone") or possibly just putting a sock over the affected paw. I can't imagine a cat leaving a sock on his paw for very long, but some cats might be fine. Another preventative might be using something nasty tasting, like Bitter Apple. Acupuncture may also ease the itching and help a granuloma heal.

The best solution is to try to determine what specifically is causing the problem. Your veterinarian may suggest skin and/or blood tests to determine the allergen.

An allergic cat can benefit from more frequent bathing.

LITTER PROBLEMS

If your cat is having allergic reactions, look at your cat litter. If you're using a scented litter, try switching to an unscented product, one that's relatively dust-free.

It is natural behavior for a cat to use his claws.

Declawing used to be very common, but now it is strongly discouraged. A declawed cat is more likely to bite and may have litter box problems in addition to chronic pain for life.

Declawing, or *onychectomy*, is amputation, which is major surgery. The last bone of each toe is removed, and the tendons, nerves, and muscles are severed. It's like cutting off each of your fingers at the last joint. Nicholas Dodman, professor at Tufts University School of Veterinary Medicine says, "Declawing fits the dictionary definition of mutilation to a T."

A *tendonectomy* is not much better. It involves cutting the flexor tendon of each claw so that the cat is unable to expose his claws. The cat can still experience lameness and infection, and, because the cat can't extend his claws, they need to be clipped regularly to keep them from growing into the paw pads.

The American Veterinary Medical Association (AVMA) says that "declawing of domestic cats should be considered only after attempts have been made to prevent the cat from using its claws destructively or when clawing presents an above normal health risk for its owner." In other words, either teach your cat to use scratching posts or resort to the soft nail covers that prevent scratch damage.

Both California and Rhode Island have laws prohibiting landlords from requiring declawing as a condition for renters, and California cities West Hollywood, Los Angeles, San Francisco, Burbank, Santa Monica, Berkeley, Beverly Hills, and Culver City, as well as Denver, Colorado, all have laws against declawing.

Countries that have banned declawing or that consider it extremely inhumane and only advisable in extreme cases are Australia, Austria, Belgium, Bosnia, Brazil, Denmark, England, Finland, France, Germany, Ireland, Israel, Italy, Macedonia, Malta, Montenegro, Netherlands, New Zealand, Northern Ireland, Norway, Portugal, Scotland, Serbia, Slovenia, Sweden, Switzerland, and Wales.

Instead of having your cat declawed, teach him appropriate scratching behavior.

35 Dental Health

Cats have thirty teeth. In the wild, they keep their teeth clean by chewing on bones and sometimes on grass. Giving your pet cat the occasional raw bone and having crunchy kibble available can help him keep his teeth clean, but they may also need your attention.

Cats don't usually get cavities the way people do, but they are prone to periodontal disease, so keeping your cat's teeth clean should be a part of your routine. Plaque can build up on a cat's teeth, and that plaque will eventually harden into tartar that will continue to build up on tooth surfaces. That tartar can cause gum abscesses, and bacteria from those abscesses can circulate through your cat's bloodstream and cause illnesses such as pneumonia, heart disease, or liver or kidney problems. Guard your cat's health by brushing his teeth regularly.

Start brushing your cat's teeth when he is a kitten. It's great if you can do it every day, but even two or three times a week is helpful, and once a week is better than nothing. Start by wrapping your finger in gauze and rubbing your finger over your cat's teeth and gums. It might help to dip your finger in tuna water or use a dab of kitty toothpaste, which come in flavors that your cat will enjoy. Never use toothpaste made for humans. They are too foamy, and since cats can't be taught to "rinse and spit," they tend to swallow the toothpaste, and fluoride is dangerous to them if swallowed.

Once your cat accepts your gauze-wrapped finger, you can advance to a toothbrush. You can use pretreated tooth wipes, a small plastic brush that fits over your finger, or a special toothbrush that looks much like your own. There are even "double" toothbrushes that brush both sides of the teeth at once.

Your cat's not going to brush his teeth on his own, so give him a hand.

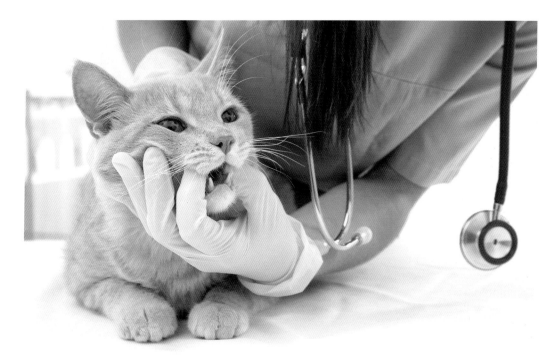

Your vet will look at your cat's teeth during check-ups, but don't neglect them in between visits.

As you clean your cat's teeth, look for any issues that may need attention. If your cat's breath is bad or smells different than it normally does, he may have a problem with his teeth. If he is drooling or pawing at his mouth, if he has trouble eating hard kibble, or he doesn't want to play with his toys, it may be time for a veterinary visit.

Even if you brush your cat's teeth regularly, your veterinarian may recommend a professional cleaning. That's not surprising—we humans brush and floss but still rely on our dentists to do a more thorough job of cleaning than we can do at home.

During a professional cleaning, your veterinarian will anesthetize your cat, remove any tartar buildup, and clean and polish your cat's teeth. If your cat has any broken or cracked teeth, your vet will pull them at this time. Before the cleaning, your veterinarian may run a blood test, especially if your cat is older. This is a safety precaution to make sure your cat won't have any problems with the anesthesia.

Dental health is just as important for your cat as it is for you. Safeguard your cat by making teeth-cleaning a regular part of your routine.

Cats, in general, are fairly healthy creatures, and many indoor-only cats live well into their upper teens or even their twenties. It's good to know what your cat might be predisposed to and how to recognize various symptoms, but if you have a wellness check with your veterinarian once a year, you probably don't need to worry too much. The following list is for information, not to frighten you out of owning a cat.

Cutaneous Mastocytosis

Cutaneous mastocytosis, otherwise known as cutaneous mast cell tumors, may be benign or may be cancerous. They are most commonly seen in Siamese and Sphynx cats, but if you notice any abnormal growth on your cat, have it checked by your veterinarian.

Feline Infectious Peritonitis

Feline infectious peritonitis (FIP) is incurable and almost always fatal, but the good news is that it's relatively rare and is more common in places where there are multiple cats, such as in shelters and catteries. The virus, which is a mutated form of the feline coronavirus, affects cats under two years old and cats ten years old and older. The virus is shed in saliva and feces, and cats can get it by either ingesting or inhaling it.

Kittens infected with coronavirus will have very mild symptoms, but they may develop FIP weeks, months, or years later. Symptoms include fever, lack of appetite, and weight loss.

There are two forms of FIP: wet and dry. With wet FIP, fluid collects in the abdomen or, occasionally, around the heart. The cat will have trouble breathing and will generally die within a week. With the dry form, symptoms are those associated with kidney or liver failure, neurological problems, or ocular problems. A cat may survive longer with the dry form of FIP but will eventually die.

There is a vaccine for FIP, but it is of limited value. The best way to protect your cat is to keep him from coming in contact with a cat who has coronavirus. Keeping your cat indoors will prevent him from meeting an infected cat that is roaming. Also clean his dishes and litter boxes daily.

FIP is most likely to affect young cats and seniors.

Glaucoma

Glaucoma is a condition in which the pressure in the eye increases to the point where it presses on the optic nerve, leading eventually to blindness. Primary glaucoma, which is relatively rare, is most often seen in Burmese and Siamese cats and will affect both eyes. Secondary glaucoma may affect either one or both eyes and may be caused by an infection or an injury to the eye.

Since the blindness is gradual, you may not notice a difference in your affected cat's behavior, but as the pressure builds, you may notice that one eye appears larger than the other, that one or both eyes look cloudy, or that your cat is squinting. As the pressure increases, so does the pain, so you may notice your cat pressing his head against objects, trying to relieve the pain.

While there is no cure, there are medications to relieve the pressure. Eventually, though, the eye may need to be removed.

Hereditary Myopathy

Hereditary myopathy is an inherited disease in Sphynx and Devon Rex cats, so if either of these is your breed of choice, ask the breeder if a DNA test has been done on the parents of your prospective kitten.

Hereditary myopathy affects muscle function. Signs of weakness can occur between three to twenty-three weeks of age, but the cat stabilizes by about nine months of age. Affected cats tire easily and may collapse. They may have problems

The Siamese is one of the breeds most affected by primary glaucoma.

chewing and swallowing, which can lead to choking and breathing difficulties as well as respiratory infections, all of which can lead to death.

Hip Dysplasia

Hip dysplasia is relatively rare in cats, but it does occur. Heavier-boned cats, such as the Maine Coon, have higher rates of hip dysplasia; in fact, approximately eighteen percent of Maine Coons are affected. Hip dysplasia is hereditary and more likely to be seen in purebreds and in females.

If you notice that your cat is not as active as he once was; if he has difficulty rising; if he is reluctant to run, jump, or climb; or if he's "bunny hopping" or otherwise seems to have pain in his hip joints, have a veterinarian check him.

Large-breed cats, such as the Maine Coon, are more susceptible to hip dysplasia.

In severe cases, surgery can correct the problem. In milder cases, controlling your cat's weight and offering an anti-inflammatory may be enough to keep your cat comfortable.

Hypertrophic Cardiomyopathy

Hypertrophic cardiomyopathy (HCM), which causes a hardening of the heart muscle, is the most common form of heart disease in cats and the number-one cause of sudden death, especially in cats between the ages of two and ten. An echocardiogram can confirm whether a cat has HCM, and there is a genetic test to identify affected cats and carriers, but there is no treatment and no way to prevent the condition.

Injection-Site Sarcoma

While it is rare, cats are more prone to injection-site sarcomas than other animals. These sarcomas are aggressive, so, if you notice anything abnormal at an injection site, see your veterinarian immediately. Sometimes a cat will have a small lump at an injection site that is merely a reaction to the shot, and it will disappear within a week or two.

Because of the chance of a problem at the injection site, many veterinarians give shots in the legs or even the tail. Then, if cancer develops, amputation of tail or leg may save the cat's life.

This does not mean you shouldn't give your cat vaccinations, but it does mean that

you might want to talk to your veterinarian about which shots are essential. For example, rabies is a required vaccination, but others may be optional. Some vaccines can be given intranasally, so that might be a solution. Another option is to run blood titers, which test for antibodies and the cat's level of immunity.

Lysosomal Storage Disease

Lysosomal storage disease is a lack of the enzymes that a cat needs for proper metabolism. Products that would ordinarily be eliminated by these enzymes get stored in the tissues, usually in the nervous

The Korat is among the breeds most at risk for lysosomal storage disease.

system. Kittens may be born normal but show symptoms in the first few months. An affected kitten may have balance or vision problems, seizures, and/or fainting spells. Cat breeds most likely to have this disease are the Persian, Siamese, Korat, domestic shorthair, and Balinese. While it can be treated initially with proper diet and careful monitoring of activity, the disease is progressive and fatal. Fortunately, it is also very rare.

Patellar Luxation

Patellar luxation is a fancy way of saying that the cat's kneecap occasionally pops out of place. When this happens, your cat will limp or hop. Generally, the kneecap will go back into place on its own, but if it happens frequently, or if the kneecap doesn't go back into place, the condition may require surgery to correct it.

Polycystic Kidney Disease

Polycystic kidney disease (PKD) is a hereditary condition that causes degeneration of the kidneys and eventual kidney failure. There is no cure. It can affect one or both kidneys, and symptoms may include excessive thirst, excessive urination, vomiting, weight loss, weakness, and high blood pressure. Generally, no signs of the disease appear until the cat is older, between seven and ten years of age, but it may appear earlier. Persians and Persian crosses are more susceptible than other breeds. Ask your breeder if her breeding stock has been tested.

The striking eyes of the Abyssinian may be affected by PRA.

Progressive Retinal Atrophy

Progressive retinal atrophy (PRA) affects the rods and cones in the retina and eventually leads to blindness. Loss of vision usually begins with night blindness and progresses from there. There is no cure. PRA is more prevalent in Abyssinians and Abyssinian crosses, but the good news for all cats is that there is a genetic test. Ask the breeder if her stock has been tested.

Pyruvate Kinase Deficiency

Pyruvate kinase (PK) is an enzyme needed by red blood cells that enables them to use energy. Cats deficient in PK have intermittent anemia and may also be lethargic or may have jaundice, pale gums, and/or an enlarged abdomen. Fortunately, PK deficiency is caused by a recessive gene, and DNA testing can determine whether a cat is normal, a carrier, or affected. Ask your breeder if she's had this test done.

Ringworm

Ringworm is not a worm but a fungal infection that eats keratin, the main substance in hair and nails, and is the most frequent skin problem affecting cats. Ringworm may attack the claws, which become pitted, develop scaly bases, and may become deformed. On the body, ringworm can cause areas of hair loss, broken hair, scaling or crusty skin, and dandruff.

If your veterinarian suspects ringworm, she will take hair and skin scrapings. If ringworm is the diagnosis, she'll prescribe both a topical and an oral medication. If your cat is a longhair, your veterinarian may want to clip the coat and may also suggest bathing your cat twice a week with a medicated shampoo. Treatment can take anywhere from several weeks to several months.

While ringworm in a healthy cat might resolve itself, it can take almost a full year, during which time your cat will have bare patches of skin that will increase his risk of skin wounds and other types of infection. Also, ringworm can be passed from a cat to another pet or a human. The sooner it's treated, the better.

If possible, keep the cat away from other pets and keep him in rooms that are easy to clean. Daily vacuuming or damp

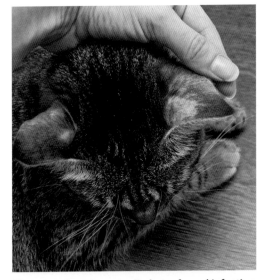

Ringworm is not a parasite but a fungal infection. This cat has hair loss on his ear due to ringworm.

mopping will help minimize environmental contamination. The ringworm spores may remain dormant for up to eighteen months on combs, brushes, food bowls, and bedding, so, where possible, use a solution of one pint chlorine bleach in a gallon of water to kill the spores.

Urticaria Pigmentosa

Urticaria pigmentosa is fairly common in Sphynx and Devon Rex cats and looks a bit like an outbreak of pimples. Outbreaks come and go, and they may be triggered by allergies. The condition is controlled with prednisolone and essential fatty acid supplements.

> ### DID YOU KNOW?
> Ringworm can be passed from a cat to another pet or a human.

37 External Parasites

Fleas

Fleas are nasty little bugs that can torment your cat with their bites. They don't spread as many diseases as ticks do, but they can make your cat's life miserable, and they're not averse to chomping on humans.

A single flea can bite your cat up to 400 times in just one day, and that same flea can produce more than 200 eggs in a couple of days. If only a tenth of those eggs grew to be adult fleas, your cat could be bitten 8,000 times a day! Besides the fact that they are sucking blood, fleas can also spread disease, and, if your cat is biting and scratching, he can cause surface wounds that can become infected. Even if your cat has only a few fleas, he may be allergic to flea saliva and will need treatment with antihistamines and/or antibiotics.

Cats who swallow fleas in the process of chewing and licking at flea bites may acquire tapeworms. Tapeworms are the least harmful of the worms that can infest your cat, and they are easily treated, but you still want to eliminate them. Tapeworm segments are visible in the stool and will look like small grains of rice. Check your cat's stool periodically for evidence of tapeworms.

Be aggressive in flea control. If you live in northern areas with cold winters, you'll have a short break from fleas. If you live in a hot, dry area, you may not have flea problems at all because it will be too dry for fleas. If you live in a warmer, wetter climate, you may be facing a year-round battle.

If your cat is scratching and you suspect fleas, turn him over and inspect his stomach, especially toward the back legs, where the fur is thinner. Push the hair against the grain. You may see a flea or two scurrying for cover. Or, you may not see fleas at all, but you may notice flecks of flea dirt. If you're not sure if what you're looking at is flea dirt or just regular dirt, collect a bit of it on a white piece of paper or paper towel and wet it. If it turns reddish, it's flea dirt.

If you don't see anything on your cat but still suspect fleas, run a flea comb through your cat's coat. Flea combs have very fine, closely set teeth that can trap fleas. Once you've determined that there are fleas, the war has begun.

Cold winters give pet owners a break from fleas.

Daily vacuuming is as effective as any spray in keeping the flea population down in the house. You can cut up a flea collar and put it in the vacuum bag to help kill the fleas. Also, change the vacuum bag frequently, or you'll be supporting a flea colony in the bag. Wash your cat's bedding frequently because that is where most of the flea eggs will accumulate. Vacuum cat-tree platforms. Combing your cat with a flea comb will also help trap the unwanted guests.

A good bath will remove fleas but will not prevent them from reinfesting your cat. There is also a pill, Capstar, which acts within thirty minutes to kill fleas on a cat. It's not a long-term preventative, but can help quickly kill fleas already on the cat. Talk to your veterinarian about short-term solutions as well as long-term protection.

Program is a monthly birth control for fleas. The fleas absorb it from your cat's blood, and the product prevents a cocoon from forming, so flea larvae never develop into adults. It does not kill adult fleas but will prevent future generations. Frontline is a topical preventative that fights fleas and ticks for seventeen days. Advantage II is another monthly topical preventative, as is Comfortis. Again, talk to your veterinarian about what will be best for your cat.

Note that there is a product called Advantix that is just for dogs. It is harmful to cats. If you have a dog and have been using Advantix, you might consider switching to a different form of protection. Some cats enjoy grooming their canine buddies, which puts them at risk of ingesting some of the Advantix.

Ticks

Ticks may or may not be a problem in your area, but, unfortunately, more and more areas that used to be almost tick-free are now seeing an invasion of the annoying little pests. And ticks are not just annoying. They can transmit deadly diseases to your cat.

Topical preventatives protect your cat from fleas and ticks for several weeks.

The tiny deer, or black-legged, tick, *Ixodes scapularis.*

If your cat is an indoors-only cat, ticks shouldn't be a problem unless you have dogs who might bring some ticks indoors. If you, your cat, or your dog tend to walk through tall grass or through brush, you are more likely to pick up a tick or two.

You can remove ticks gently with tweezers or put alcohol on them. Never use a cigarette or anything else that will burn. Undoubtedly, that would get the tick's attention, but you are also likely to burn your cat. If you don't think you can remove the tick properly, or you don't want to try, have your veterinarian do it for you. The important thing is to check your cat on a routine basis if ticks are a problem in your area, and do not leave them on your cat. Ticks can be hard to find, so be patient and thorough.

Ticks can transmit diseases that can affect your cat; these include Lyme disease, ehrlichiosis, anaplasmosis, Rocky Mountain spotted fever, cytauxzoonosis, tularemia, haemobartonellosis (also called feline infectious anemia), and tick paralysis.

Lyme disease is spread by the deer tick, also called the black-legged tick. Symptoms include lameness, lethargy, and lack of appetite. While it is possible for a cat to contract Lyme disease, according to the Cornell Feline Health Center at the Cornell University College of Veterinary Medicine, there is no documented case of a cat ever having Lyme disease outside of a laboratory setting. There is no Lyme vaccine for cats, but if your cat ever shows symptoms, or you've removed a tick and are worried about Lyme disease, contact your veterinarian. When treated early with antibiotics, Lyme disease can be cured with no lasting effects.

The brown cat tick spreads ehrlichiosis, another disease rarely seen in cats. Symptoms include fever, lack of appetite, depression, weight loss, runny eyes and nose, nosebleeds, and swollen limbs.

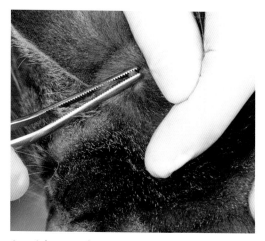

Any ticks must be removed immediately by either you or your vet.

The black-legged, or deer, tick also spreads anaplasamosis. Symptoms include fever, lack of appetite, stiff joints, lethargy, vomiting, diarrhea, and possibly seizures. It is easily treated with antibiotics.

The American cat tick, the wood tick, and the lone star tick spread Rocky Mountain spotted fever. This is seen more frequently in dogs, but cats can also contract it. Symptoms may include fever, lameness, lack of appetite, vomiting, and diarrhea. Some animals may develop pneumonia or liver or kidney damage. It is treated with antibiotics.

Cytauxzoonosis is seen more in the southern central and southeastern United States. This is a nasty disease that can kill your cat in as little as a week. Symptoms may include anemia, depression, fever, difficulty breathing, and jaundice. Drugs and intravenous fluids may help, but they are not guaranteed to work, and there's no vaccine.

Tularemia, also called rabbit fever, is fairly rare. In addition to being transmitted by ticks, mosquitoes, and fleas, your cat can catch the disease he kills and eats a rabbit or rodent. Symptoms are a high fever, swollen lymph nodes, and nasal discharge. It is treated with antibiotics.

Haemobartonellosis, or feline infectious anemia, can be transmitted by both ticks and fleas. The disease attacks the red blood cells, and symptoms include weakness, loss of appetite, anemia, jaundice, and possibly a fever. In severe cases, blood transfusions may be needed along with antibiotics.

ANEMIA

If you suspect anemia, look at your cat's gums—they will be pale instead of a healthy pink color.

Tick paralysis is another tickborne disease that is rare in cats. Caused by a toxin from the tick, the disease's symptoms include weakness in the hind legs that progresses to the front legs and an increased difficulty breathing and swallowing.

To protect your cat from ticks and to minimize his risk of contracting these diseases, reduce the tick habitat in your yard by cutting back overgrown shrubs. Ticks like dark, moist places, so get rid of any dead wood or piles of lawn debris. Consider using a tick preventative from your veterinarian; there are chewable tablets as well as topical products. While antibiotics may cure a disease, preventing that disease is the better course of action.

Ear Mites

Ear mites are most common in kittens and outdoor cats. These tiny, eight-legged parasites eat wax and oils in a cat's ear canal. Symptoms include scratching and rubbing the ears, head shaking, and hair loss. The cat's ear(s) may become inflamed, and there may be a strong odor from the ear(s). Left untreated, the ear canal can fill with a dark, waxy secretion.

The cat may develop skin infections from scratching and digging at his ears, which can cause him to break blood vessels. These hematomas frequently require surgery to correct. Additionally, the mites, if left untreated, can lead to an ear infection called *otitis externa*, which starts in the outer ear but can progress through the middle and inner ear and damage the ear drum itself, affecting both the cat's hearing and balance.

So, if you suspect ear mites, make an appointment with your veterinarian. If your cat has ear mites, your vet will likely clean the ear and then offer eardrops and/or an oral antibiotic, depending on whether there is infection. After the infestation has cleared up, your veterinarian may recommend a regular schedule of ear cleaning, which you can do yourself at home if your cat allows it.

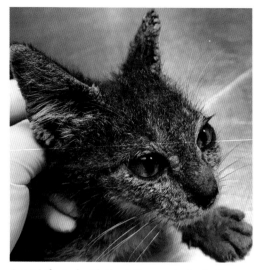

A cat infected with the feline equivalent of scabies.

Mange Mites

Mange is very rare in cats, but it's worth a mention. There are two types of mange. The first, notedric mange, is also called feline scabies. It causes a severe skin infection that starts at the head and spreads. These mites are highly contagious, but the good news is that they are extremely rare. According to Mar Vista Animal Medical Center's website, most veterinarians never see a case of mange in a cat, unless they are in a "regional 'hot bed' of infection. . . . Southern California is such a hot bed, and the infection is relatively common." Ask your veterinarian whether you live in a risky area for mange.

Demodectic mange mites are even more rare. They aren't contagious but, if present in sufficient numbers, may affect hair growth around the eyes, lips, and ears.

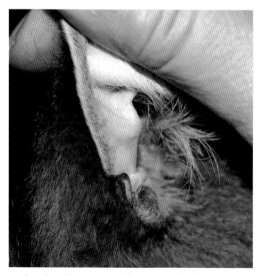

Make checking your cat's ears part of your regular routine.

A first-aid kit is something everyone should have, and many items that belong in a feline first-aid kit are similar to those found in a kit for humans. However, there are some things that are specific to cats and there are items in a human first-aid kit, that can harm, and possibly kill, a cat.

It's always best to check with your veterinarian before giving your cat any oral medication that wasn't specifically prescribed for him. As an example, there is no home remedy that can safely be used to induce vomiting in a cat. If your cat has eaten something poisonous, get to your veterinarian immediately. If that's not possible, call the ASPCA Animal Poison Control Center, 888-426-4435, or the Pet Poison Helpline at 855-764-7661. Both charge a fee, so have your credit card ready.

Getting back to the first-aid kit, if you don't have a special kit, designate one shelf in a cupboard for your cat's first-aid supplies so you know right where they are in an emergency and there's no time wasted. If you travel a lot, carry a small kit in your car as well—even just some antiseptic and gauze can be helpful.

Consider including a muzzle in your first-aid kit. Even the gentlest family pet may bite when in pain, and if you're worried about being bitten, you can't concentrate on helping your cat. Most pet-supply stores carry special muzzles for cats. While you might be able to fashion a muzzle out of gauze, most cats' muzzles aren't long enough for a person to do this easily. Never muzzle an unconscious cat or one who is having any trouble breathing.

Another thing to remember is that a first aid kit is not a substitute for veterinary care. For minor injuries, they're fine, or to help stabilize your cat for a trip to the vet's, but a first aid kit is not a do-it-yourself kit for broken bones, heavy bleeding, or deep cuts or puncture wounds. Because cats are harder to treat orally and because more medicines are toxic for them, if possible, consult your veterinarian even before administering first aid.

Here are some useful first-aid supplies:

- **ACTIVATED CHARCOAL:** Give this orally if your cat has eaten something that you suspect is poisonous because the charcoal helps neutralize the poison. This is not the same as the charcoal you use to barbecue. As your pharmacist for the right kind of charcoal.

- **ADHESIVE TAPE AND/OR VETERINARY WRAP:** Adhesive tape will work to hold a bandage or splints in place, but it will also pull your cat's fur. Veterinary wrap won't stick to fur. Pet-supply retailers carry it, or maybe your veterinarian will sell you a roll.

- **ANTIBIOTIC OINTMENT:** Use this on scrapes and shallow cuts. It's also good for hot spots. I use a triple antibiotic cream, which you can find at any drug store.

- **ARTIFICIAL TEARS:** If you've been somewhere dry and windy, artificial tears can soothe your cat's irritated eyes.

- **BENADRYL:** Give one milligram per pound of body weight for allergic reactions, such as to a bug bite or bee sting. For most cats, half of a 25-milligram tablet will work.

- **COTTON BALLS:** You can use cotton balls or pieces from a roll of cotton for applying salves or liquid topical medications.

- **GAUZE:** A roll of gauze can secure dressings. Various sizes of gauze pads are also good to have for covering wounds.

- **HEMOSTATS AND/OR TWEEZERS:** Both of these items can be used to remove splinters or larger pieces of debris that may be in a wound.

- **HYDROCORTISONE OINTMENT:** This is useful if your cat has bug bites, or a rash.

- **HYDROGEN PEROXIDE:** You can use hydrogen peroxide to clean and disinfect a wound, but soap and water is probably better. Do not use hydrogen peroxide to induce vomiting.

- **PROVIABLE-KP:** This is a brand-name product that contains kaolin and pectin, the ingredients that help stop diarrhea. Kaopectate used to contain these two ingredients, but it no longer does, and the new formula is dangerous to cats. Do not use Kaopectate or Pepto-Bismol with your cat.

- **RUBBER GLOVES:** They're not a necessity, but they can make dealing with something messy a bit more pleasant.

- **SCISSORS:** Use scissors to cut gauze and veterinary wrap and for trimming fur away from a wound.

- **SYRINGES (ORAL):** It's much easier to administer medicines with an oral syringe than with a spoon. Stock 3-, 6-, and 12-centimeter sizes.

- **THERMOMETER:** Your cat's normal temperature will be between 99.5°F (37.5°C) and 102.5°F (39°C). This should go without saying, but you'll need to take your cat's temperature rectally, not orally.

Gauze comes in handy for wrapping wounds.

PAINKILLER CAUTION

Never give your cat aspirin, ibuprofen or acetaminophen. All three can be fatal to cats!

- **VETERINARIAN'S PHONE NUMBER:** Keep your vet's number, as well as the number of your local emergency clinic, with your first-aid supplies.

- **VETERINARY FIRST-AID MANUAL:** A manual can be helpful when you don't know what to do in emergency situations.

If you'd prefer some holistic choices for first-aid care, here are a few that might be useful.

- **ALOE VERA:** Gel from the aloe vera plant can help relieve pain and itching from hot spots, insect bites or stings, and other skin irritations. It has a bitter taste, so it might help discourage your cat from licking or biting at an injured area. Use it in moderation, and never let your cat chew on or eat the actual plant, as it is toxic.

- **ARNICA GEL:** Use arnica gel for sprains and bruises.

- **CALENDULA GEL:** This gel encourages healing of scrapes and shallow wounds.

- **CAYENNE PEPPER:** Powdered cayenne pepper can be used to stop bleeding.

- **COMFREY OINTMENT:** This is another good product for minor scrapes and injuries. Use it sparingly, for emergencies only, and don't use it for long periods of time.

- **RESCUE REMEDY:** This mixture of five Bach flower essences is used to treat shock, collapse, and trauma.

39 Hairballs

Hairballs result from cats' self-grooming.

Hairballs can be icky, especially if you step on one or if your cat leaves one in your slipper, but they typically are not dangerous. Hairballs are formed when your cat swallows fur. Usually, the fur will pass through the digestive tract, but sometimes your cat will hack up a hairball. The more your cat grooms himself, the more likely he is to form a hairball or two.

A cat's tongue is covered with tiny barbs that help rasp meat off a bone, and they act as a comb when a cat grooms himself. Unfortunately, all of those barbs point back toward the throat, so once the hair is on the tongue, the cat will swallow it; he can't spit it out.

Brushing your cat, especially if he has long hair, can help reduce the number of hairballs, as can adding a teaspoon of olive oil to your cat's food once or twice a week. Some people speculate that grain-based foods affect a cat's digestive system so that hair doesn't easily pass through. There are commercial products on the market to help combat hairballs, but some veterinarians are reluctant to suggest them because they are petroleum-based. Check with your veterinarian before you use such a product.

Sometimes, instead of being vomited up, a hairball may cause an obstruction. If your cat continues to gag, retch, or vomit without producing a hairball, or if he has a lack of appetite, is lethargic, or has constipation or diarrhea, make an appointment with your veterinarian.

nternal parasites are those organisms that live inside a host—in this case, your cat— taking their nourishment from their host. They can weaken and even kill a cat if left untreated.

Worms are one of the most obvious types of internal parasites. Worms that can infect a cat include roundworms, tapeworms, hookworms, whipworms, lungworms, and heartworms.

Roundworms

Roundworms are not generally a threat to healthy adult cats, but they can be life-threatening to older cats and kittens. Cats get roundworms by ingesting roundworm eggs, which may be present in the soil or may be transferred to a cat by earthworms, cockroaches, rodents, or birds. All of these are hosts only to the eggs. The eggs don't hatch until they are inside a cat, dog, or human.

Some of the worms may live in a dormant state in a host's body and then come out of dormancy during a pregnancy. When this happens in a cat, the worms are passed to the kittens through the placenta or through the milk once the kittens are born and nursing. Because a kitten who is heavily infested with roundworms could die, it is essential to deworm kittens, and, because the roundworms mature at different rates, kittens need two or three treatments at two- to three-week intervals. The first deworming should be done when the kittens are two to three weeks old.

If you have an indoor/outdoor cat, you'll want to either regularly deworm him or have your veterinarian test fecal samples several times a year. While you may not notice any symptoms in a healthy adult, symptoms may indicate a serious problem in an older cat. Symptoms include vomiting, abdominal swelling, coughing, and lethargy.

Roundworms are among several parasites that a mother cat can pass to her kittens.

To help prevent the spread of roundworms to humans, keep children away from areas that might be contaminated. Remove feces from the litter box daily and, when cleaning the litter box, add bleach to the water. The bleach doesn't kill the eggs, but it makes them easier to rinse away. After cleaning, rinse the litter box thoroughly and wash your hands thoroughly as well.

Hookworms

Hookworms are more common in dogs than in cats, but cats can get them. An adult cat can become infected by hookworms in two ways. The first way is by ingesting any eggs that may be in the soil. Often, a cat will ingest eggs while grooming his feet. The second way is when larvae burrow through the skin and migrate to the intestine. As with roundworms, kittens can be infected when nursing.

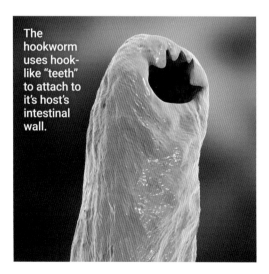

The hookworm uses hook-like "teeth" to attach to it's host's intestinal wall.

Hookworms use their hook-like mouths to attach to the intestinal wall and suck blood. In an adult cat, if you notice digested blood in the stool (the stool will be dark or black), weight loss, and/or a dull, lifeless-looking coat, have your vet test a stool sample for hookworm eggs. Another symptom might be itching, especially of the paws.

Because blood loss, especially in kittens, can lead to life-threatening anemia, deworming is important. If your cat does have hookworms, two worming treatments two to three weeks apart will eliminate them. Many heartworm preventatives also prevent hookworm.

Whipworms

Cats rarely get whipworms, but it is possible. Your cat may have bloody diarrhea or show signs of dehydration, anemia, or weight loss if he's got whipworms. Whipworm eggs can live in the soil for years, so if your cat ever has whipworms, it's likely that he'll have them again. Whipworm eggs can be detected by testing a stool sample.

Tapeworms

Your cat can get tapeworms if he's eaten an infected rodent or ingested flea larvae. Tapeworm eggs don't show up in fecal exams, but if your cat has tapeworms, you may notice small white segments of the worms, rather like grains of rice, either in your cat's stool or in the fur around your cat's rectum. Tapeworms are one of the least harmful worms that can infect your cat,

but they are still parasites, so you'll need to contact your veterinarian for the proper medicine to eliminate them.

Lungworms

Unlike the other worms mentioned, lungworms do not live in the intestines but in the lungs. Cats who hunt rodents and birds are at risk of getting lungworms. Symptoms are coughing and shortness of breath, caused by worm larvae that are laid in the cat's airway. They also cause a mucus accumulation. If the infestation is left untreated, damage to the airways can lead to emphysema, fluid build-up in the lungs, and pneumonia. Eggs that are coughed up or passed in the feces may be eaten by birds, rodents, or other pets, continuing the cycle.

To determine if your cat has lungworms, your veterinarian may need to run several tests. Since it can take up to a month for the eggs to show up in the feces, your veterinarian may do a tracheal wash, which may show the presence of larvae. She may also x-ray the lungs to see what else might be causing coughing and to check the lungs' condition.

Lungworm treatment is possible, but it may take up to eight weeks of a medication. If there are secondary infections, your cat may also need antibiotics and/or corticosteroids for inflammation.

Tapeworm segments appear like grains of rice in a cat's stool.

Heartworms

Cats are not as susceptible to heartworm as dogs are, but they can still be infected, and heartworms can lead to death. Heartworms are transmitted through mosquito bites, and, while mature heartworms do live in the heart, there are no adult worms in many infected cats. The danger for cats is the damage caused by the immature worms, which affect the pulmonary arteries leading to the lungs and the air sacs in the lungs themselves. Veterinarians call this heartworm associated respiratory disease (HARD).

An infected cat may vomit, have diarrhea, have trouble breathing, and may cough. In severe cases, the cat may die suddenly. Because the symptoms could be indicative of some other disease, your veterinarian will check a blood sample to see if there are antibodies to the parasite and will test for heartworm proteins.

While dogs can be cured of heartworm, there is no cure for heartworms in cats. The cat may recover on his own and can be helped with intravenous fluids as well as by certain drugs and antibiotics.

Prevention is the key to keeping your cat safe from heartworms. Eliminate breeding grounds for mosquitoes by making sure there are no areas of standing water in your yard. Talk to your veterinarian about the best heartworm preventative for your cat. There are both oral and topical preventatives on the market, and many of them also protect against other parasites.

Heartworm is transmitted by mosquitoes, which can be hard to avoid.

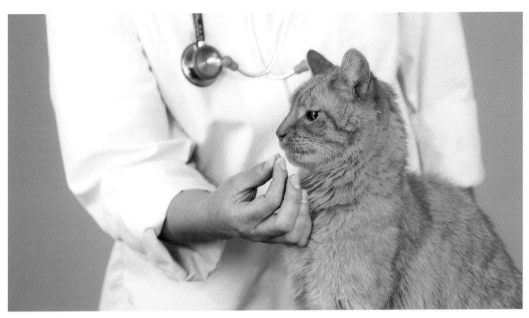

Offering your cat a pill and expecting him to take it probably won't work.

You've probably seen humorous instructions for how to give a cat a pill. The instructions start by telling you to hold your cat gently but firmly, and they end with the house in a shambles, the cat on top of the bookcase, the humans on the way to the emergency room, and pills scattered all over the floor. The instructions for giving a dog a pill follow: Wrap pill in cheese. Throw at dog.

While it may be harder to give a cat a pill than a dog, it doesn't have to end in trauma for everyone. It's easy to ignore the potential difficulty until your cat needs some medicine, but if you work on how to give a pill before the cat needs it, you can save all parties a lot of stress.

The first cat I ever gave pills to was perfectly amenable to taking them in a soft treat. Your cat may be the same way, but don't wait to find out until it's necessary. Find some soft treats that are small and tasty. There are many soft treats on the market, and there's even a soft paste that you can mold around a pill. Maybe your cat adores a bit of soft cheese or meat. You can use anything that is small and soft and hides the pill. Don't use large pieces that your cat will need to chew. You don't want him crunching into the pill and spitting it out.

Get your cat used to you touching his face and mouth. While your cat may voluntarily take a hidden pill, you want to make sure he gets it down, and that means popping it into his mouth so he'll swallow.

Start by gently stroking your cat's face and throat. Offer him a treat or two. When he's used to this, hold him and gently squeeze his

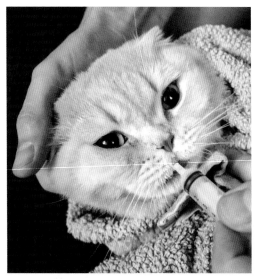

An oral syringe works for liquid medications or for giving the cat some water.

Give one or two treats without the pill, then give the treat with the pill, and then give another treat. To help soothe your cat's throat and help him digest the pill, give your cat a bit of water. If he'll drink some tuna water, that's great. Otherwise, use a small oral syringe (the type used to administer medication) to give him some water.

Don't give your cat more water than he can swallow. A teaspoon or less is probably plenty. You don't want any of the water to enter the lungs, which could lead to serious problems, including pneumonia. If your cat will let you, pull his lower lip out to the side and squirt the water into that pocket. It will be easier for the cat to swallow, and you won't risk water going into the lungs.

An alternative to pills can be compounding. If you have a pharmacy near you that does compounding, they can turn certain medications into tasty liquid that your cat will happily lap up. Talk to your veterinarian about the possibility of compounding. Not all medicines can be compounded, and compounds cost more than pills, but it might be worth it to make sure your cat takes the medicine he needs.

cheeks, using your thumb and forefinger, so that he opens his mouth. Tip his head back so that his nose is pointing at the ceiling. With the other hand, place the tiny treat at the back of his tongue and close his mouth, gently stroking his throat. If he doesn't swallow, softly blow across his nose. He should lick his lips after he's swallowed. If you're not sure of this technique, ask your veterinarian to show you when bring your cat in for an examination.

When the time comes to actually give a pill, line up several treats. Wrapping your cat loosely in a towel may make it easier for you to hold him, but the operative word is loosely. Don't wrap your cat up so tightly that he panics. The idea is for everyone to be calm, not terrified.

Your veterinarian can show you how to use an oral syringe to administer medication.

The term *neutering* technically applies to both castrating (removing the testicles) a male and spaying (removing the ovaries or the ovaries and uterus) a female, but the term *neutering* has come to refer to males and *spaying* to females.

Spaying or neutering your cat has many pluses. First and foremost, it prevents unwanted litters that frequently end up in shelters or are otherwise abandoned. A neutered male will be less likely to mark with urine, and, if he's an indoor/outdoor cat, he'll stay closer to home and be less likely to get into fights with other males.

Unspayed females may also mark surfaces with their urine and may become very vocal. Cats, unlike dogs, aren't limited to being in season twice a year. An unspayed female cat may come into season every one to three weeks. If she has not mated during that time, she will go out of season for one to two weeks and then be receptive to mating again. In warmer climates, this is a year-round cycle. Further north, the winter months may signal a break in heat cycles.

A cat's gestation period is about nine weeks long, and the average size of a litter is two to six kittens, but there can be more. A female cat can become pregnant again anywhere from one week to two months after the litter is born.

The vocalizations of both males and females, whether they are in love or fighting, can be pretty annoying. It's loud and unpleasant. In *A Tramp Abroad*, Mark Twain blames it on grammar:

"You may say a cat uses good grammar. Well, a cat does—but you let a cat get excited once; you let a cat get to pulling fur with another cat on a shed, nights, and you'll hear grammar that will give you the lockjaw. Ignorant people think it's the noise which fighting cats make that is so aggravating, but it ain't so; it's the sickening grammar they use."

Kittens are adorable, but so many end up in need of good homes.

Silver female and brown tabby male Siberian cats.

In males, neutering prevents prostate problems, including prostate cancer and testicular tumors. With females, spaying decreases the risk of cancerous mammary tumors and eliminates any chance of pyometra, which is a life-threatening infection of the uterus. Pyometra can occur any time, and the symptoms are not always easy to spot; if not treated, it will kill the cat.

Traditionally, cats were spayed or neutered at around six months of age, but veterinarians are increasingly performing these surgeries at a younger age. Many female cats are fully mature at four months old. At shelters, kittens may be spayed or neutered as young as six weeks of age.

On their website (*www.catvets.com*), the American Association of Feline Practitioners cites a study indicating that cats who are neutered or spayed early have a decreased chance of developing asthma, gingivitis, and hyperactivity. On the negative side, the cat may show increased shyness. Otherwise, there seem to be no adverse effects of early spaying or neutering.

Unless you plan to become a serious breeder, with all of the work that it entails, spay or neuter your cat. Trust me—life will be easier for both of you.

You've got the right kind of litter box and the right kind of litter. Your cat can easily get to the box, as well as into and out of it, but all of a sudden, he's not using the box anymore. Or he's using it a lot, but not much is happening. Your cat may have a urinary-tract infection and, according to petMD (*www.petmd.com*), urinary-tract disease is one of the most common reasons cats are surrendered to animal shelters.

Feline idiopathic cystitis, sometimes called idiopathic feline lower urinary tract disease (IFLUTD) or feline urologic syndrome, is an inflammation of the bladder that can lead to a cat's straining when urinating. There may be blood in his urine, and urinating may be painful. That pain may be the reason your cat isn't using his litter box—he is avoiding the litter box because he is associating the pain with the box. You may also notice your cat licking his genital area to ease the pain.

Wet food can help prevent urinary-tract infections.

A urinary-tract infection can lead to stones in the bladder or a urethral plug. The latter can be fatal because it totally blocks the cat's ability to urinate and thus rid the body of toxins.

If you notice your cat having any trouble urinating, or if he is suddenly avoiding his litter box, make an appointment with your veterinarian immediately. If your cat can't urinate, he could die within twenty-four to forty-eight hours. Your veterinarian will test both urine and blood samples and may also take X-rays or do an ultrasound.

If the urethra is plugged, your cat will be sedated and the blockage removed. Your veterinarian will insert a catheter so she can flush the bladder and keep it empty to help reduce inflammation. She may perform surgery to permanently enlarge the opening of the urethra to help prevent future problems. Your cat may also need surgery if he has bladder stones. Additionally, your vet will probably prescribe antibiotics to help fight the infection.

To help prevent urinary-tract infections, feed high-protein, low-carbohydrate wet food. If you are feeding only dry food, add twice the amount of hot water as you have food and let the food totally absorb the water before feeding.

If your cat is ignoring the litter box, there could be a medical reason behind it.

Initial vaccines are an important part of keeping your kitten healthy. Even indoor cats should receive initial vaccinations. An indoor kitten or cat could escape despite your best efforts, or you could bring a disease into the home yourself. Some diseases are airborne, so even being indoors may not protect your cat. If you decide that one cat isn't enough, that second or third cat could be carrying a disease, depending on where the new cat came from.

Indoor cats can still be at risk for certain diseases.

The combination vaccine is a core vaccine that protects against feline rhinotracheitis, feline calicivirus, and feline panleukopenia and is abbreviated FVRCP. Vaccinations can start at six weeks, and kittens are vaccinated once every three to four weeks after that until they reach sixteen weeks or older. Most veterinarians start the shots at eight weeks, with boosters at twelve and sixteen weeks.

Feline viral rhinotracheitis (FVR) is an upper respiratory infection that is very contagious and can cause death in kittens. It is transmitted through direct contact, so it's important to clean surfaces regularly. Symptoms include coughing, sneezing, nasal discharge, fever, and loss of appetite. The vaccine can weaken the severity of the disease and may reduce viral shedding, but it doesn't prevent the infection.

Feline calicivirus (FCV) is another virus that exists in in the environment, so a cat doesn't need to come into direct contact with a sick cat to contract the virus. Symptoms include loss of appetite, eye and nasal discharge, trouble breathing, lameness, fever, and ulcers in the mouth, on the nose or lips, or around the claws.

Feline panleukopenia (FP) is sometimes called feline distemper or feline parvo. It's highly contagious and affects kittens most frequently. The virus infects and kills cells in the bone marrow, lymph nodes, and intestines, as well as in developing fetuses. The virus is everywhere in the environment but may be more concentrated in kennels, animal shelters, and feral cat colonies. Kittens, sick cats, and unvaccinated cats are the most susceptible. While an infected cat usually only sheds the virus for a few days (some cats can shed the virus in urine and stools for up to six weeks), the virus can survive for up to a year in the environment.

The virus can be spread through bedding, food dishes, or the hands and clothing of a person who has had contact with an infected cat. The virus is resistant to many disinfectants, so an unvaccinated cat should not be allowed into an area where an infected cat has been.

Symptoms of FP include depression, loss of appetite, high fever, vomiting, diarrhea, and dehydration. In kittens, the virus can also damage the brain and the eyes. Kittens under eight weeks old generally don't survive FP. Even older cats are likely to die unless they receive supportive care, such as fluids and essential nutrients. Because infected cats are more susceptible to bacterial infections, antibiotics may also be needed.

Most kittens receive their first set of vaccinations around eight weeks of age.

The other vaccine essential for all cats is the rabies vaccine. There is no cure for rabies once contracted, and it is fatal. The rabies shot is generally given at twelve weeks, but check with your veterinarian. Laws vary from state to state.

Some states require that cats be vaccinated for rabies, while others do not, but even if your state doesn't require it, and you plan to keep your cat indoors, it's still a good idea to get him the rabies shot. It's easier than you think for a bat to get indoors, and if your cat catches and kills it, he could be infected with the rabies virus. Remember, you don't get a second chance with rabies.

There are some noncore vaccines that you can discuss with your veterinarian to determine whether or not your cat should receive them. There are vaccines for feline leukemia (FeLV), feline immunodeficiency virus (FIV), and Chlamydophilia felis. There are also vaccines for feline infectious peritonitis (FIP) and Giardia but these are not widely given. In fact, the American Association of Feline Practitioners lists the FIP vaccine as "not recommended." FIP is a deadly disease, but it's hard to test for because its virus is a mutated form of the feline coronavirus, which is present in about 90 percent of all cats. FIP is almost always fatal.

Giardia is an internal parasite generally contracted from contaminated water or from eating the cysts, which can live in damp ground for several months. The main symptom is smelly, greenish diarrhea that may also be bloody. The diarrhea may be intermittent. Your veterinarian can examine

Vaccinations protect against certain diseases that can be passed between pets.

a stool sample to determine if your cat has *Giardia*. If he does, your veterinarian will prescribe a drug—either fenbendazole or metronidazole—in pill form for five to seven days. Because both of these drugs are bitter, and it may be hard to get them into your cat, look into getting them flavored at a compounding pharmacy.

FeLV is viral and can be transferred from the mother to the kittens. Some veterinarians recommend this vaccine for all kittens; others recommend it only for kittens at risk. According to Cornell University, FeLV is one of the most common infectious diseases in cats and can affect a cat in several ways, the most common of which is cancer. It may also cause various blood disorders and may create immune deficiency, allowing for secondary infections.

The virus can be transferred from a bite, during grooming, or from contact with saliva, urine, feces, or milk of infected cats. Since the vaccine will not protect a cat 100 percent, preventing exposure is important. Keeping your cat indoors is a good start. Don't bring in another cat until that cat has been tested for FeLV. Cats with FeLV have a life expectancy of about two and a half years.

Generally, the vaccine for FIV is reserved for cats at high risk and, since the vaccine will not protect all cats, prevention is important. Cat bites are the major way that the disease is spread, so keeping your cat indoors (as well as spayed or neutered) will help keep your cat safe.

FIV attacks the immune system, allowing normally harmless bacteria, viruses, or fungi to cause illness. An FIV-positive cat may show slow, progressive weight loss. The cat may have bouts of illness alternating with spells of good health, or the cat's health may just progressively worsen. The average life expectancy of an FIV-infected cat is five years.

The vaccine for *Chlamydophila felis* is only given in multiple-cat environments where the infection is known to exist. Symptoms are conjunctivitis and respiratory problems.

Find a vet who makes your family feel comfortable.

If you've taken in a stray, you'll want to have him checked out immediately by a veterinarian, and that may mean a trip to the first clinic that has an opening. If you've decided to get a cat from the local shelter, a breeder, or even a neighbor, and you know the kitten or cat's veterinary history, you'll have some time to consider which veterinary clinic you want to go to and how far you're willing to travel. However, no matter where you get your cat, an early veterinary exam is a good idea. You'll need to continue your cat's vaccinations, at the least, and catching any health issues early can mean that they will be easier to treat.

While proximity can be a very good thing when you need veterinary care, check out your area's practices to see if there's a felines-only doctor within a reasonable distance. While you can get good care in a mixed practice, the atmosphere may be a bit calmer in a practice that caters just to cats. Visiting a veterinarian can be stressful enough without adding barking dogs to the mix.

Of course, that feline practitioner may be thirty miles away, and you may not mind the drive for routine visits, but what happens in an emergency? If you need to get to your veterinarian in the middle of a blizzard, maybe someone located a bit closer to you would be a better choice, unless there is a conveniently located emergency clinic.

Another consideration is how many doctors are in the practice. If you go to a practice with just one veterinarian, that doctor will get to know you and your cat very well, but if you need to go to another practice in an emergency, your cat's medical records won't be available. In a practice with multiple veterinarians, you may not have the same individual rapport with one doctor, but all of the doctors will have access to your cat's medical records. Another benefit to a practice with multiple doctors may be in the way they handle emergencies. With several doctors, someone is most likely "on call" after hours and on weekends. If you choose a practice with just one veterinarian, ask how she handles emergencies. Does another practice cover for her, or is there

an emergency veterinary clinic in your area? Ask these questions now so that you're not wasting time trying to find a vet in a crucial situation.

If possible, visit the office before you make your decision. The waiting room should be clean, and the staff should be friendly. Separate areas for cats and dogs are a plus, but not a must.

You may need to make that initial appointment before you can make a final decision on the best vet for you and your cat. If everything meets your approval, but you just don't feel comfortable with a particular

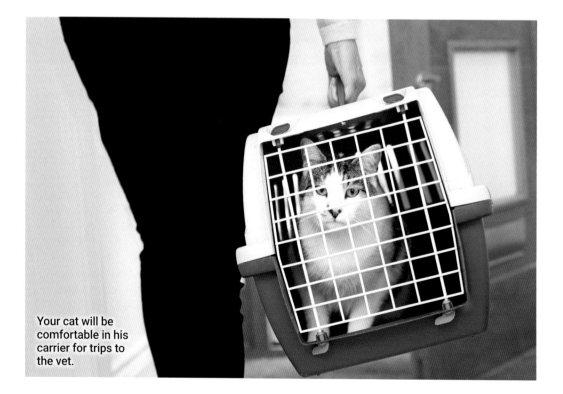

Your cat will be comfortable in his carrier for trips to the vet.

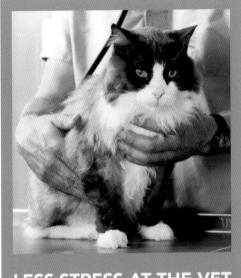

LESS STRESS AT THE VET
Some veterinary practices strive to create a calming atmosphere for their patients, with treats, soothing music, and special considerations for handling each animal so that the visit is less stressful for the pet.

with just one visit, remember that you'll often be dealing with the office staff and vet techs as much as you're dealing with the doctor. Does the staff treat you and your cat with consideration? Do they take your concerns seriously? I want to know that the staff will make every effort to get my cat the attention he needs if it's a true emergency.

The following example from my own experience happened with my dog, but the same thing applies to cats. Years ago, we had just moved to a new area. My dog had broken a nail so that it stuck out at a right angle. It wasn't life-threatening, but he was in pain, and it was difficult for him to walk. I called a veterinary hospital not far from our home and was told that they could see me in five days. I called another practice located a bit farther away. They said to bring the dog in immediately. Guess which practice has had my business for more than twenty years?

Another consideration is the specific kinds of treatments you may want available for your cat, like acupuncture or chiropractic. Maybe you're more comfortable with a vet who uses a traditional approach, or maybe you like the idea of a holistic vet—or maybe you'd like to see a vet who incorporates holistic methods into traditional medicine. Find out what each veterinary practice offers. Maybe a practice doesn't have a chiropractor on site but has a close relationship with a chiropractor who will work on your cat. It's up to you to discuss with your vet just what kind of care you want for your cat.

vet, find another one. You and your vet will be partners in keeping your cat healthy. You need to feel comfortable asking questions, and you need to have confidence that your vet is giving your cat the best care possible. If you have doubts, find another practice.

The same goes for the staff. While you might not be able to get a feel for the staff

46 Whiskers

Never cut, trim, or interfere in any way with your cat's whiskers. Whiskers on a cat are not like whiskers on a human. Cats rely on their whiskers to supply them with information, and a cat without whiskers is at a huge disadvantage because he's lost a very vital sense of touch.

The theory is that whiskers developed to help nocturnal and aquatic animals hunt in the dark. Seals and walruses have very prominent whiskers, as do rats. Dogs have whiskers, but they are not as highly developed as those of cats. A dog can function if you cut his whiskers. If you cut a cat's whiskers, you've effectively crippled him.

Whiskers, or vibrissae, are longer, stiffer, and more deeply embedded than regular fur. The whiskers on each side of the cat's nose and on the upper lip are the obvious ones, but there are also shorter whiskers over each eye, along the jawline, and on the backs of the front legs.

At the end of each whisker is something called a propriocepter that sends signals to the brain and nervous system. This makes the whiskers receptive to even the smallest change in the environment. Whiskers can respond to vibrations in the air caused by prey, helping the cat follow erratic movements instantly. The whiskers help

A cat's whiskers help him gather important information.

the cat gauge whether or not he can fit into a specific space and help the cat measure distance when he is jumping up or down.

A frightened cat's whiskers will likely be bunched up and flat against his face. On a startled, excited, or hunting cat, the whiskers will point forward.

It's fun to watch a cat use his whiskers and to try to understand what information he's receiving. Just remember how important they are to the cat and leave them alone.

Do not cut or otherwise alter your cat's whiskers in any way.

PART VIII

Your Cat and Your Health

Studies have shown that animals can positively affect our health. Whether your pet is a cat or a dog, people with pets have lower blood pressure, lower cholesterol levels, and decreased feelings of loneliness. If you put a harness on your cat and walk around the neighborhood, you'll have the added benefits of exercise and socialization. No one's going to be able to resist your cat, which means people will stop to chat. Even Sheldon Cooper of *The Big Bang Theory* benefits from just hearing about a cat. When he's tired or ill, he demands that someone sing him the "Soft Kitty, Warm Kitty" song, and he feels calmer and more relaxed.

Sometimes, cats help indirectly. Many smokers will stop smoking when they learn that their secondhand smoke can harm their cats.

Cats can also be therapy animals. If your cat has a calm, outgoing personality, you can take him on visits to hospitals, nursing homes, or schools. You can be, but you don't need to be, certified by an organization to visit with your cat, but the institutions themselves may have requirements, like proof of

Cats can be companions and stress relievers.

vaccinations. Make sure that your cat's nails are trimmed before any visit. Your cat should also be comfortable wearing a harness and being on a leash.

If you'd like the training and support of a therapy-animal organization, visit the Pet Partners website at *www.petpartners.org*. They offer liability insurance coverage to their certified animal-assisted therapy teams. To qualify, cats must be at least one year old and have lived with you for at least six months. Cats on a raw diet are not eligible.

If you decide you'd like to visit places with your cat, and your cat has the temperament for it, remember to keep an eye on your cat. You don't want your cat to become tired or stressed. Be ready to remove your cat from any situation in which he's becoming stressed or anyone is in any danger.

Besides being generally good for people's health, cats can be emotional-support animals. Emotional-support animals can live in "no-pets" housing and are exempt from any pet deposits that housing may require. An emotional-support animal doesn't have to have any special training, but for your cat to legally be considered an emotional-support cat, a therapist must write a letter prescribing the need for the animal.

While the Americans with Disabilities Act does not legally recognize cats as service animals, cats may unofficially be as useful as a recognized service animal. Unfortunately, not having legal status can prevent a cat from entering places that prohibit animals.

Janiss Garza, writing for the Fear Free website (*www.fearfreehappyhomes.com*) in February 2018, tells the story of a woman who, after a car accident, developed a brain clot that would cause her to pass out. She has trained five cats over the years to help her. To quote Garza, "Her current pair . . . can call for help, drive Audra's wheelchair, push her out of the shower, and bring her small items, such as the phone. One of them always accompanies Audra in public and can alert her before she passes out, so she can get to a safe place."

Even if you don't need your cat for specific medical reasons, no one can deny the feeling of calm that comes from holding a purring cat on your lap.

You or a family member may be allergic to cats, and you may wonder if there's a cat that will not trigger these allergies. The fact is that, while some cats may be hypoallergenic, which means they are less likely to trigger an allergy attack, no cat of any breed is totally nonallergenic.

Cats produce a protein in their saliva called Fel-D1. This is the protein that causes allergic reactions and can leave a person with runny, itchy eyes or restricted breathing. When a cat grooms himself, the saliva gets on the coat and causes dander. Shed skin and hair may eventually reach the nose and eyes of an allergic person. It has very little to do with whether a cat is longhaired or shorthaired.

Some cats produce lower levels of Fel-D1 than others, and this can make them an acceptable choice for someone allergic to cats. The Siberian has a long coat but lower levels of Fel-D1 than any other breed of cat.

The Sphynx, with almost no hair, also has low levels. Besides the low level of Fel-D1, there's no airborne hair to carry any saliva, and, because they benefit from regular baths, they are less likely to spread dander. The Russian Blue is another breed that produces lower levels of Fel-D1, and its plush coat resists shedding.

An allergic person might try a Cornish Rex. While it doesn't have lower Fel-D1 levels, it has a silky coat that doesn't shed much, so the amount of the allergen in the air and on surfaces is lower.

A cat allergy produces sneezing, runny eyes, itchiness, and other symptoms.

The hairless Sphynx may be a good choice for those with cat allergies.

The Balinese is another cat that produces a lower level of Fel-D1, so, even though it has a longer coat, it may be an appropriate breed for someone with an allergy to cats. The Balinese originated as a Siamese mutation, and the Siamese is one of the cats listed on the PetMD website (*www.petmd.com*) as a possible cat for those with allergies. The site also lists the Bengal, Burmese, Colorpoint Shorthair, Devon Rex, Javanese, Ocicat, and Oriental Shorthair as potential choices.

None of these suggestions is a guarantee. For example, one of my friends is allergic to cats, and her allergy symptoms are much worse around short-coated cats, with the Siamese causing the worst reaction. She fares better around longhaired cats, even those with normal levels of Fel-D1.

So, use the cats mentioned here as a guide, but remember that no cat is nonallergenic, and even those considered hypoallergenic might not be in certain cases. If you have an allergy to cats, but you still want one, talk to your doctor about ways to control your symptoms. One way might be to limit textiles that can trap and hold dander and hair, such as carpets, rugs, draperies, and textured upholstery. Another might be to designate certain areas of the home as "cat-free," especially the bedroom. HEPA-filtered vacuum cleaners can also help. Still another solution might be regular allergy shots. If your allergy symptoms include a runny nose and itchy eyes, there may be shots that you can get regularly to keep those symptoms under control.

The Ocicat may not cause problems for an allergic owner.

The Cornish Rex's low-shedding coat means less allergens around the home.

49 Cat-Scratch Fever

Cat-scratch fever, or cat-scratch disease, is caused by a specific bacterium, and, while most cats who catch this disease show no signs of illness, they can pass the disease on to humans. Cats get infected from flea bites and from flea dirt getting into wounds. Cats who bite and scratch at fleas can get the infected dirt under their nails and on their teeth. If such a cat bites or scratches a person and breaks the skin, the person can get cat-scratch disease.

Three to fourteen days after the bite or scratch, the person may develop an infection at the site of the broken skin. The area may swell and become red, with raised lesions that may contain pus. The person may have a fever, have a headache, and be tired. Lymph nodes near the bite or scratch site may become swollen and tender.

Most of the time, a person gets better with no treatment other than a pain reliever and warm compresses on the wound site. Children under five years old and people with weakened immune systems may have more serious problems and should consult their physicians.

A bite or scratch from a cat can spread the bacteria that causes cat-scratch fever.

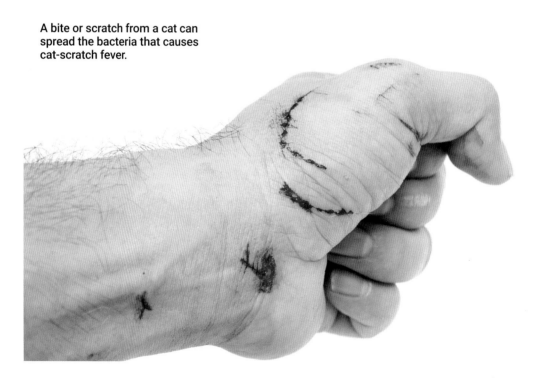

Toxoplasmosis is caused by the parasite *Toxoplasma gondii*, and a healthy person's immune system keeps the parasite from causing illness. Pregnant women and those with compromised immune systems need to be cautious. If you are pregnant, you might not have any symptoms of toxoplasmosis, but your baby could be affected, usually within the first year of life, by vision problems or brain damage.

Many people think that if a member of the household is pregnant, the family must get rid of the cat, but this is not true. While toxoplasmosis can be a threat, with just a few safety precautions, the family cat can stay right where he is.

Cats become infected with the parasite by eating infected rodents, birds, or other small animals. Cats and kittens can shed the parasites in their feces for as long as three weeks after they've been infected. That means that the *Toxoplasma* parasite can be in litter boxes, sandboxes, and other soil. Indoor cats, who do not have the opportunity to hunt and kill small prey, are not likely to carry the parasite.

Whether your cat is an indoor or outdoor cat, if you are pregnant, play it safe and avoid changing the litter box. If you must do it, the Centers for Disease Control recommend wearing disposable gloves and washing your hands with soap and water after you've finished with the litter box. Someone should change the litter box daily because the parasite doesn't become infectious until one to five days after it is shed.

Avoid stray cats, especially kittens, and don't get a new cat while you are pregnant.

If you have an outdoor sandbox, keep it covered (this is always a good idea). If you garden, wear gloves and always wash your hands afterward.

The *Toxoplasma* parasite can also be present in undercooked meat, so feed your cat commercial food rather than raw to prevent contact with contaminated meat. Because fruits and vegetables may have come in contact with contaminated soil or water, wash and peel them before eating, or make sure they are cooked.

With just a few simple precautions, you and your cat can welcome a happy, healthy baby.

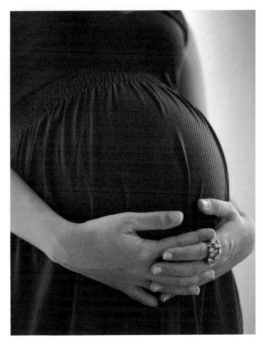

Pregnant women must take precautions against toxoplasmosis for their babies' safety.

PART IX

Things to Do with Your Cat

Can cats be trained? Yes, definitely. Should you bother? Again, yes, definitely. There is no downside to proper training. With training, you can modify or end any problem behaviors that your cat may have already learned, such as counter surfing. Training also increases the bond between you and your cat. Further benefits of training are that it's mentally stimulating for the cat and helps to reduce stress.

Certified animal behavior consultant Steve Dale notes some other reasons why training your cat is a good idea. Says Dale, "Cats mask illness. The better you know your cat, the more apt you are to notice even the slightest change in behavior. Plus, cats enjoy learning if you keep it fun. And, more than 50 percent of all cats are obese. Training provides some activity, and it also keeps the cat's brain active."

If you've taught your cat to come when called and to willingly get into a cat carrier, it could save your cat's life if there's a disaster and you need to evacuate. It can also make a trip to the veterinarian's office faster and much less stressful for both you and the cat.

Even if you teach your cat only one thing, that one thing could save his life. A friend of mine has two cats, and she taught them to sit on command. One day, one of the cats got out of the house. As my friend went after the cat, she realized that she probably couldn't catch her, so she told the cat to sit. The cat obeyed, giving my friend time to reach her and pick her up.

A simple cue like "sit" could save your cat's life.

With a clicker (a small, handheld noisemaker), some treats, and patience, you can teach your cat positive behaviors and create a closer bond with your feline friend. A good book to help you get started is *Naughty No More* by Marilyn Krieger. Following advice in this book, you can teach your cat positive behaviors and work through such problem as counter surfing, furniture scratching, and inappropriate elimination. Or get almost any book by Karen Pryor, which will tell you what you need to know about clicker training.

Clicker training relies on the specific noise of the clicker as a marker for a desired behavior. The animal receives a reward—usually food, but sometimes a toy or petting—after the marker. You can use a word, such as "good" or "OK," as the marker, but the advantage of the clicker noise is that it is always the same. There's no variation and no confusion because you are using the clicker only when training.

You can use clicker training in three ways to get the behavior you desire: luring, capturing, and shaping. With *luring*, you take a treat and use it to lead, or coax, your cat into position. An example is holding a

The clicker makes a sound that serves to "mark" the desired behavior, telling the cat that a reward is forthcoming.

treat slightly back and over your cat's head to encourage him to sit. As he sinks back and into a sit position, click and give him the treat. Keep the treat low and click and treat quickly because, unlike dogs, a cat won't wait for the treat but will use his claws to try to get it.

To *capture* the sit, you wait patiently with clicker and treat until your cat sits on his own, at which point you click and treat. You use *shaping* to add more precision to a behavior. For instance, your cat sinks back almost into a sit, and you click to mark that movement. Eventually, you no longer click for the partial sit but only when the cat's entire rear end hits the deck. Then, if you want your cat to sit with his front paws side by side in front of him, you begin to click only when his paws are in that position.

CHARGING THE CLICKER

To teach the cat that the sound of the clicker means a reward, you "charge" the clicker by clicking and treating rapidly several times in a row so that the cat associates the sound with a treat.

Ideally, when first starting to train, you should work somewhere with no distractions. If your cat is watching birds at the feeder, he's not going to be paying attention to you. If possible, train with the cat on a raised surface. This will save your back and, because most cats like heights, your cat will be very comfortable on a chair or table. Use a mat or piece of carpet to prevent him from slipping.

Make your treats small. You are not feeding a meal. Use something special that your cat loves. Thin-sliced deli turkey, torn into tiny bits, works well. To begin, teach something that your cat is already inclined to do. Here are some examples from my experience working with cats at our local animal shelter.

First I worked with Claudia, a lovely gray and white tabby who was very relaxed and happy, with her tail up and purring nonstop. I tried luring her into a sit with some turkey, but she would just reach up with her paws, trying to snag the turkey. I decided to just wait until she sat, capturing the sit with a quick click and treat. The problem was that she just wanted to rub back and forth and purr.

The next day was more of the same. I could capture the occasional sit, but Claudia mostly just wanted to rub back and forth against my legs and purr, which was delightful but not helpful for my experiment. Remembering that it helps to teach natural behaviors, I decided that if Claudia's inclination wasn't to sit, maybe I could capture movement. I placed two chairs about eighteen inches apart, and Claudia

Use small treats as training rewards.

was delighted to jump from one to the other, especially with a turkey reward.

The next day, Claudia came to the door of the cat colony and eagerly scooted through the door to join me. She willingly jumped on request and, by the end of the session, she was also learning to sit nicely for her turkey.

In the senior colony, I worked with Icarus, a large black and white cat. In ten minutes, Icarus knew that if he wanted turkey, he had to sit neatly with all four paws on the floor. We made progress, but the next time I visited the shelter, I found out that Icarus had been adopted. I was thrilled for him and his new family, but it meant starting over with another cat.

Fortunately, another cat volunteered. Gage, a small black cat with big green eyes, already knew about the turkey because I'd given him some when I was working with Icarus. By the end of the session, he was on his way to consistent sits.

These three cats had no attachment to me, but it didn't take any of them very long to understand the connection between specific behaviors and a tasty treat. Your own cat will probably learn even faster. Remember to work for just a few minutes at a time. You don't want to overdo it and end up with a bored or tired cat. Three to five minutes at a time is long enough.

Start with something your cat is inclined to do anyway. When I realized that Claudia enjoyed movement, that became our starting point, and then we moved on to learning to sit. If you have a Ragdoll, he may never be excited about jumping, but you could teach him to roll over or maybe give you a "high five."

Whatever you decide to teach your cat, both of you will enjoy the process.

DID YOU KNOW?

You can teach your cat to wave a paw or give a high-five.

Capture your cat's natural behavior as you teach him to jump up on cue.

The only thing more fun than buying toys for your kitten is playing with them. It's not only fun to play with your cat, but it's good for him. Play teaches your kitten to be social and friendly, it develops his hunting skills, and it increases his brain size. Play mimics hunting and exploring and, says Dr. Gary Landsberg, an animal behaviorist in Thornhill, Ontario, "If you have an indoor cat, and you don't give [him] toys or provide opportunities to play, you are going to have a fat, lazy cat, or a cat with behavior problems." A cat needs to act on his natural urges, and toys are a safe way for him to do that.

Social play is when your kitten plays with other cats or with you. You can play with your kitten with toys, and you can make a game out of training with tasty treats. Playing with and handling your kitten helps him bond with you and get used to people. When you have visitors, your well-socialized kitten will be more likely to say hello than hide under the bed.

Toys on a string are interactive fun for cat and owner.

BIG BRAINS

While there have been no direct studies of cat brains, Dr. Katherine Houpt, retired animal behaviorist, formerly of Cornell University's College of Veterinary Medicine, says that, based on studies with rodents, play probably results in a larger brain, with more neural branches, resulting in a smarter cat. Play frequently with your kitten, and you may end up with the feline equivalent of Einstein!

Object play is when your cat plays by himself with balls, bits of paper, and things like cardboard boxes and paper bags. Just remember that different cats react differently to different toys, so it's up to you to figure out what your cat most enjoys.

Before you start your first play session with your furry pal, pay attention to a few guidelines. First, never play a game in which your cat is chasing your hand. Don't wiggle your fingers or move your hand so that the cat will chase it. Don't play that game under the covers, either. Cats are programmed to chase and kill small wiggly things, and a bite or scratch from a cat can be painful. Also, you don't want your cat to think your hand is a toy that he can bite or scratch at will. Even if a blanket protects your hand, you don't want your cat pouncing on you every time you're in bed. It may seem cute at first, but—trust me—it will get old fast. Use appropriate toys that your cat can catch and bite.

GOOD KITTY!

Another benefit of play with your kitten is that he will expend his energy in safe play and thus will be less likely to engage in destructive behavior, such as climbing up the drapes, for example.

Supervise play between your cat and small children. Children can be too rough with a pet, and while some cats will tolerate more than others, don't risk injury to your child or your cat. Teach children to stroke gently and not to pull on tails or legs. Also supervise play so that you can separate cat and child if you recognize that the cat is getting stressed and may be ready to bite or scratch.

Never let a child corner your cat. Any animal that feels trapped may panic and attack. Call an occasional "time out" so that, if your cat would like to end playtime, he can do it without anyone getting hurt.

A kitten may not be used to keeping his claws sheathed during play, so stop play when the claws come out. It's OK if your kitten is clawing or biting an appropriate toy, but if he tries to bite or scratch anyone, make a hissing noise and stop playing. Ignore the kitten for a few minutes before returning to play. Your kitten will soon learn that biting or scratching means an end to the fun.

There are many household items that make good cat toys, but plastic bags are not one of them. A kitten could easily suffocate, and any cat, if he chewed and swallowed the plastic, could end up with an obstruction that requires surgery.

Laser lights can be great fun, but they can also be dangerous. Never flash the light directly into your cat's eyes. If your kitten is extra fast, and you're not as coordinated as he is, a flashlight might be safer.

Kittens love to play with pieces of yarn or string, but supervise this play. Swallowed string can be deadly, and if a kitten gets tangled in yarn or string, he may panic and hurt himself.

Make sure that there are no small parts on a toy that a kitten or cat could chew off and swallow.

Your cat will enjoy the movement and sound of a small ball with a bell inside.

If the toy has a potentially dangerous part, remove that part before giving the toy to your kitten. Pick up and put away any toys that could be potentially dangerous if not supervised. It's fun to drag or swoop a toy attached to a string, but remember that the string can be deadly. Put it away when you are not playing with your cat.

Toy mice are always popular, but you may have to hunt to find just the right kind for your cat. Some cats prefer furry mice while others like shiny mice or mice wrapped in raffia. Most kittens adore catnip toys, but not all cats like catnip, so you'll have to experiment.

Many kittens love toys on a string or a wand, especially if the toy is made of fur or feathers. Instinct makes it hard for a cat to resist a moving object that could be a potential meal. On days when you just don't have the time or energy to tire out your kitten, tie a feathery or furry toy to the end of a long string, attach the other end to your belt, and let the toy bounce and drag behind you as you move about the house. Your kitten will enjoy the chase and get exercise without having your undivided attention. Just

Puzzle toys engage a cat's mind.

remember the rule about string: put the toy out of reach when you're finished using it.

Your kitten may love glittery balls and tiny balls that contain jingle bells, especially if you have a breed that enjoys a game of fetch. If you don't have a ball, a crumpled-up piece of paper will often suffice. Some stores carry ping-pong balls filled with rice, and these make a sound that your kitten may find fascinating.

In fact, ping-pong balls seem to top the list of toys that kittens love. One kitten and a ping-pong ball or two in the bathtub (minus the water) equals an exciting hockey game. Or, take a large cardboard box, put some holes in the sides for the kitten to jump in and out of, and fill the bottom with ping-pong balls. Your kitten will love burrowing into the balls and batting them around the box.

WATER PLAY

Maine Coons and some other breeds enjoy playing in water, so if your water-lover has fabric catnip-stuffed toys, you may need to replace them when they've had one dip too many.

If you have a cardboard box but you're short on ping-pong balls, just give your kitten the empty box. You can turn it into a tunnel, make holes in the side, or just leave it as is for your kitten to hide in. Paper (never plastic) bags are another favorite toy that won't cost you a cent. Just make sure that if the bag has handles, you cut them off before giving the bag to your cat. Those handles could get wrapped around your cat, causing him to panic. Many kittens love to bat around bottle caps, or your pet may enjoy the empty cardboard tube from a roll of toilet paper.

No matter what kind of toys you use, leave out only two or three at a time and put the rest away. Rotate the toys every two or three weeks to keep them fresh and interesting for your cat. If your cat enjoys catnip, throw the toys in a bag of catnip to add a little zest to an old toy.

With a little imagination, you'll find a lot of toys and games for you and your kitten to enjoy. If you keep things safe and supervise play, everyone in your family, including the cat, will enjoy playtime.

DIY PLAY

Toys don't have to be expensive. Instead of buying a toy, tie a bit of fabric or fake fur to a string, attach the string to a stick, and bounce the toy around so that your kitten can leap at the "prey." If you don't mind a little mess, or if you have an enclosed porch, gather up a handful of autumn leaves and watch your kitten pounce and roll.

Cats can find myriad ways to have fun with paper bags.

I love cat trees. Cat trees combine both horizontal and vertical scratching surfaces with assorted shelves and nap areas for your cat. A basic model will just have two or three carpeted shelves and a sisal-covered post, but more expensive models may have multiple shelves, a hammock or two, boxes with holes for access, and toys begging to be swatted. A cat tree gives your cat a safe, comfortable place to be up high, and that may help keep him off bookcases and other shelves that you'd rather keep for books or knick-knacks. Your cat may also prefer the platforms on the cat tree to your furniture, which can help keep your furniture fur-free. Cat trees with multiple levels also work well when you have more than one cat.

A cat tree can cost several hundred dollars for a fancy model, but no matter what size you get, or how much you spend, make sure it's solidly built and stable. You definitely don't want a cat tree falling over on your cat or when your cat is using it.

If you don't find cat trees as wonderful as I do, or you just don't have the space for one, you can install a small cat-sized shelf level with a window. This gives your cat a perch up off the floor, and he can enjoy watching whatever might be going on outdoors. Put a bird feeder in front of that window, and your cat's got his own nature show.

A good cat tree combines multiple climbing and scratching surfaces.

Be sure that you choose a sturdy cat tree that won't tip over.

54 Exercise Wheels

If you have only one cat, and he's an indoors-only cat, consider getting an exercise wheel. This is a large, solid wheel, similar to the exercise wheels in hamster cages. It's basically a treadmill for cats, and it's a great way for your cat to burn off energy. The only drawback might be the size, but if you can position it near a wall, it won't take up too much floor space.

Exercise wheels are expensive, but you won't be putting your cat through college or buying him pricey sneakers, and the wheel will likely last for the lifetime of your cat. You will spend a couple hundred dollars to buy one, but there are do-it-yourself options if you're handy and would like to save money.

Your cat might enjoy expending some energy in an exercise wheel.

Cats have the grace, reflexes, and natural athleticism for agility competition.

Agility

The sport of cat agility is growing by leaps and bounds, literally, and is a great way for you and your cat to have fun. In agility, cats maneuver over, under, and around various obstacles. This sport helps develop coordination, balance, speed, power, and reaction time in a cat. Both The International Cat Association (TICA) and the Cat Fanciers Association (CFA) offer competitive classes at many of their cat shows.

Competitions offered by International Cat Agility Tournaments (ICAT) are a feature of many TICA shows. While ICAT was started by two TICA judges, it is a separate organization. An ICAT agility course will include four bar or hoop jumps, a tunnel, a cat walk that is long enough for four foot touches, weave jumps or weave poles, and a table jump, where the cat jumps across a gap between two tables.

At CFA shows, agility is open to any cat, whether pedigreed cats, house pets, or shelter cats. Cats that have been declawed or that have a physical deformity may also compete.

In CFA agility, the ring contains ten obstacles: four hurdles (one with one bar, one with two bars, one with three bars, and one with four bars), two tunnels, weave poles, stairs, and two hoops. Handlers are allowed to use toys to encourage their cats, but no food of any kind is allowed. The course runs counterclockwise, and timing starts when the cat's paw touches the first article and ends when he completes the last obstacle.

Each cat completes three timed runs, and the best score is chosen. In case of a tie, the cats involved will each run another course to determine the winner. Cats receive fifteen points for each obstacle completed, and any cat who completes all of the obstacles in the correct order within the time limit (4 minutes and 30 seconds) will receive bonus points. Rosettes are awarded to the top five competitors, but all competitors who complete the course correctly get points toward titles.

Nosework

Why should dogs have all the fun? Nosework is an organized competitive activity for dogs, but there is not organized nosework for cats yet. However, you and your cat can still enjoy the challenge of this activity on your own, as many other cats and owners do. You can find many videos online of cats putting their noses to good use.

CFA TITLES

There are four agility titles offered in CFA agility:

AGILITY COMPETITOR (AC): Awarded for successfully completing the course within the time limit. Once a cat earns this title through CFA, all other agility runs by that cat will be considered for points.

AGILITY WINNER (AW): Awarded at 500 points.

AGILITY MASTER (AM): Awarded at 2,000 points.

AGILITY GRANDMASTER (AG): Awarded at 4,000 points.

In nosework, a cat must locate a particular odor or odors and then indicate to his handler that he has found the correct scent. In the dog world, dogs must find specific scents in four different situations: exterior, interior, vehicle, and container, all in a set period of time. You might not want to do exterior work unless your cat is comfortable wearing a harness. It won't be fun if your cat runs away. If you can work with your cat outdoors, the difficulty increases, because there will be many more smells competing with the one you want your cat to find.

Indoors, you can start working with your cat in just one room. As your cat learns and gains confidence, expand the search into additional rooms.

If you're hiding scent in assorted containers, experiment. In the beginning, make things easy by using small boxes. Later, you might add more complex containers, like purses or backpacks.

Start with just one odor and work up to three or more. The scents used in canine nosework are birch, anise, clove, myrrh, and vetiver. Most pharmacies sell small vials of these scents, or you can experiment to see what scents work best with your cat. Because cat nosework is not an organized sport, you can use any scents that you choose.

If you'd like to try nosework, start by letting your cat find, and eat, treats from small open boxes. Add an odor to one of the boxes and put more treats in that box than in any of the nonscented boxes. Gradually eliminate the treats from the other boxes until only the box containing an odor has a reward. If you've worked with your cat and have trained any specific behaviors, like sit, you can add that to the game so that when your cat finds the box with the odor, he will sit (or otherwise let you know that he's found the correct box).

> Nosework is typically considered a dog sport, but cats can use their noses, too.

Sooner, rather than later, your cat will knock a toy of some kind under something, and that something will be too close to the ground for either you or your cat to reach the toy. This is when you'll reach for your yardstick.

Two of our yardsticks came from lumberyards, another came from a discount store, and a fourth is hiding in an upstairs closet. You can get one at a hardware or home-improvement store. They come in handy for many things, one of which is getting cat toys out of odd places.

Don't think that you can just ignore that item under the couch or stove, because the minute it disappears, it will become your cat's favorite thing, and he will not stop trying to reach it. You'll need to get that yardstick and rescue the out-of-reach treasure. And there's an added benefit: besides retrieving the out-of-reach item, the yardstick will bring out any dust bunnies that have grown undetected.

Sometimes, cats knock things into places where a yardstick is no help at all. If you have floor registers, the grates may have openings large enough for small cat toys. Bottle caps and tiny foil balls can get through, as can small treats.

If the treat or toy goes all the way down the heating duct, there's not much anyone can do, but if it lands on the ledge around the duct, you can pry up the register and get the treat. The cold air return, however, is a different story. That grate at our house is wooden and is firmly nailed in. If something fun or tasty falls through the grate, it's lost. That's when I start chewing gum.

I rarely chew gum, but I keep a pack for emergencies. Once I've softened up the stick of gum, I push it onto the end of a drinking straw. A thin dowel works for this, too, but a pen or pencil is likely too short. The straw easily passes through one of the grate openings, and I can gently push the gum onto the item and then draw it up and out.

If the toy is too heavy, you won't be able to rescue it at all, so you'd better hope that your cat's absolute favorite toy never slips through a grate.

PART X

Cat-Care Concerns

There are hundreds of plants that are more or less dangerous to your cat, but with just a little caution, you can keep your cat safe.

To start, if you love lilies, you'll have to give them up if you get a cat. All parts of a lily are highly toxic to your cat. If your cat brushes against a flower and gets pollen on his fur and then licks it off, he's been poisoned. He can even be affected if he drinks water that the lilies have been in. If your cat is drooling or vomiting, and you think he's been chewing on a lily, get him to your veterinarian immediately. Your veterinarian will try to induce vomiting if the cat hasn't already vomited, and she will get the cat on IV fluids to help prevent his kidneys from shutting down.

Calla and peace lilies will cause drooling, vomiting, and diarrhea, but will not harm the kidneys. Lily of the valley, while not technically a lily, affects the heart and can cause seizures or a coma.

You may also have to reconsider your holiday decorating. All parts of mistletoe—leaves, stems, and berries—are poisonous, but it's the berries that are the worst. Mistletoe berries can be fatal if your cat

BEWARE!

If you want to know if a plant is truly a poisonous lily, try to find its Latin name. Avoid any plant with the genus name *Lilium* or *Hermerocallis*.

Easter lilies, part of the genus *Lilium*, are off-limits to cats.

ingests even a few. Play it safe and buy a nice artificial cluster. They look quite real, and they eliminate a potential source of trouble. If you positively must have the real thing, make sure it's out of your cat's reach and keep an eye out for fallen berries. If your cat is vomiting, has diarrhea, has seizures, or falls into a coma, get him to your veterinarian immediately.

Holly berries can cause upset stomach, seizures, and loss of balance, so, again, play it safe and invest in some artificial holly. It will last longer and you can use it again next year.

Poinsettias have always gotten a bad rap as being poisonous, but they're not nearly as bad as mistletoe and holly. The leaves, stems, and sap can cause irritation, and, if the sap gets in the eyes, it can cause blindness. If your cat chews on a poinsettia, he could suffer from vomiting and diarrhea. You don't have to eliminate poinsettias from your

decorating scheme, but do keep them out of your cat's reach.

Even a Christmas tree can cause problems. While not specifically toxic, the needles can cause pain if a cat swallows them. Never let your cat drink from the tree stand.

I have never known anyone to decorate for Christmas with Christmas roses, but on the off chance that you do, you should know that they don't make good toys for cats. The Christmas rose can cause vomiting and diarrhea and can affect the heart.

Don't bring boxwood or yew into the house. Boxwood can cause heart failure, and yew has both poisonous berries and foliage. Eating the berries can cause cramping and vomiting. Eating the foliage can cause sudden death with no symptoms. If you have boxwood or a yew tree on your property, get rid of it before you get a cat.

The other plant I would never have in my yard is oleander. Oleander is very toxic,

Mistletoe berries are the most harmful of the holiday plants, being fatally toxic to cats.

Although it looks pretty, oleander is a real danger to cats.

and all parts of the plant are poisonous, particularly the leaves. It contains the cat toxin referred to as glycosides. Symptoms are gastrointestinal problems, heart-function problems, and hypothermia; in some cases, it can cause sudden death.

Iris, tulip, and daffodil bulbs are poisonous, but it's unlikely that your cat will intentionally dig up the bulbs, so you can enjoy the flowers without much danger. If you've purchased some bulbs to plant, don't let your cat play with them.

Apple seeds contain cyanide, as do cherry and peach pits, but, assuming your cat would even want to eat apple seeds, he'd have to consume hundreds to be poisoned. Peach pits, being larger, would be more of a threat; if swallowed, they could also cause an intestinal blockage. Again, I'm not sure any cat would want to chew on a peach pit, but make sure pits and seeds end up in the garbage and not where your cat can get them.

Rhododendron, philodendron, marigold, hydrangea, hemlock, and rhubarb can all be harmful. Another type of growth that may be harmful to pets is mushrooms. Many types are totally harmless, but many are harmful, and unless you're a student of mushrooms, you won't know the difference until it's too late. The ASPCA reports that certain mushrooms can cause kidney or liver damage or serious neurological consequences; some types may even be fatal.

If you're planning to add a new plant to your yard, ask the folks at the nursery about any parts of the plant that may be poisonous and, if so, what kind of problems they can cause.

There are too many plants that are potentially poisonous plants to list them all here, but a list of toxic plants may be found at the ASPCA's website (*www.aspca.org*). Check this list if you're planning to add a new plant (or shrub or tree) to your yard. You can also ask the nursery staff if they are aware of any dangers associated with the plant.

"POISON" IVY

Ivy can cause vomiting, diarrhea, muscular spasms, and paralysis.

58 Other Dangers at Home

Antifreeze

If your cat is an outdoor cat or has access to your garage, antifreeze could be a threat. Just one teaspoonful could kill your cat. The ethylene glycol in antifreeze is toxic to the brain, kidneys, and liver. If your cat is vomiting, walks as if drunk, has head tremors and twitching muscles, and is drinking and urinating more than usual, and you suspect he's lapped up some antifreeze, get immediate veterinary care. If your cat vomited or had diarrhea, take a sample to your veterinarian when you go. That could save time and might save your cat's life.

Antifreeze tastes sweet to animals, so they are likely to lap it up if they find it.

Aspirin and Other Pain Relievers

Cats don't metabolize aspirin the way dogs do. It can take a cat up to forty-eight hours to fully metabolize just half of a baby aspirin, so you should only ever give aspirin under veterinary supervision. Never, ever give acetaminophen, which will destroy your cat's liver and likely kill him. Never give ibuprofen, either, as it will destroy the kidneys and may also lead to death. In fact, there are very few medicines for humans that are safe for cats. Protect your cat by keeping all medicines out of reach and only using medicines approved by your veterinarian.

Bismuth Subsalicylate

It bears repeating that a cat is not a small dog. If you have a dog, you can't assume that what is safe for him is also safe for your cat. Many products that are harmless to dogs can be deadly for cats. For instance, bismuth subsalicylate, the active ingredient in Kaopectate and Pepto-Bismol, is safe for dogs but not for cats. Originally, Kaopectate was a combination of kaolin (a type of clay) and pectin, which was fine for cats. The ingredients have changed, though, making the product unsafe for cats.

Essential Oils

Essential oils are not essential to your cat, and they may even be fatal. Essential oils have become very popular, as have essential-oil diffusers that are used in the home. You may find essential oils soothing and relaxing, but your cat lacks the liver enzyme that metabolizes these oils. The higher the concentration of the oil, the greater the risk to your cat. The oil can be absorbed orally or through the skin, and symptoms of poisoning

Essential oils and diffusers have become very popular but are not recommended for use in homes with cats.

can include vomiting, drooling, tremors, respiratory distress, low heart rate, low body temperature, and liver failure.

Depending on the strength of the oil and the sensitivity of your cat, you may have to give up your diffuser. Even if you keep the oils themselves away from your pet, the odors from a diffuser can bother your cat. Your cat may develop a runny nose or eyes, may drool or vomit, or may have difficulty breathing so that he is panting, coughing, or wheezing. If your cat has any of these symptoms, get him into fresh air. If this doesn't ease the symptoms, take him to your veterinarian.

Flea and Tick Preventatives

Always make sure that the flea and tick preventatives you use are made specifically for cats. Depending on the ingredients, something made for dogs may not be safe for cats. Never let your cat chew on a flea collar, and, of course, always use the product as directed. I once overheard a woman in a veterinarian's waiting room say that she had a hard time getting her pet to swallow the flea medicine. It was not an oral medicine, but one made to be applied between the shoulder blades. Please read the directions.

Nicotine

Nicotine is very poisonous to cats. Depending on how much a cat ingests, symptoms can include vomiting, diarrhea, elevated heart and respiration rate, tremors, weakness, seizures, coma, and cardiac arrest. If you smoke, keep ashtrays clean of butts. If you chew snuff, keep the containers away from your cat.

A new danger from nicotine comes from e-cigarettes. These hold vials of a liquid nicotine solution, and that solution can also be purchased in bottles for refilling the cartridges in the e-cigarette. If a cat lapped

Keep any items containing nicotine away from your cat.

up some of that liquid, he would be getting a real jolt of nicotine. Or, if a cat spilled some on himself and then licked it off while grooming, he could still ingest a deadly amount. If you use e-cigarettes, keep them away from your cat.

Toilets

Unless you've specifically trained your cat to use your toilet as his own, keep the lid down. A kitten can easily drown in a toilet, and even an adult cat can panic and drown if there's no one around to pull him out of the bowl.

The other issue with toilets is chemical cleaners. If you use a product that continuously cleans your toilet, your cat's fur would become soaked in the chemical if he fell into the toilet. Keep the lid down.

The blue toilet water may look inviting, but it poses drowning and poisoning risks to pets.

MORE PRECAUTIONS

BLEACH: If bleach splashes on your cat, wash him thoroughly. Rinse his eyes immediately and then get to your veterinarian if the bleach gets in your cat's eyes.

LAUNDRY DETERGENT: Keep laundry detergent away from your cat. Pods can be especially dangerous because their compact size makes it easy for a cat to grab one. Spurting liquid can harm the eyes and is toxic if swallowed.

NAPHTHALENE AND PARADICHLOROBENZENE: These are both toxic. Naphthalene is a chemical found in toilet bowl deodorizers, mothballs, moth crystals, and moth cakes. Paradichlorobenzene is found in diaper-pail, toilet-bowl, and restroom deodorizers and in mothballs, moth crystals, and moth cakes.

If you're visiting family or friends on a vacation, you might be able to take your cat with you, but, sometimes, traveling with your cat just isn't practical. When you need someone to care for your cat while you're away, your main options are boarding kennels and pet sitters.

In an article by Amy Shojai on the Fear Free website (*www.fearfreepets.com*), she says that cats take from five days to two weeks to adjust to a new routine, and some cats may adjust better than others. I once owned a boarding kennel, and many cats were just fine, but I clearly remember one in particular who was very unhappy and seemed furious when his owners came to pick him up.

The Fear Free website suggests that when you go away, you pick up different scents and don't smell familiar when you return, which is why your cat may take a while to accept you again. Before you go away, Shojai suggests taking a pair of socks, rubbing them all over your cat, and then sealing them in a plastic bag. When you return home, wear those socks, which will smell like your cat and will reassure him that, yes, you are family.

Your cat will be comfortable at home if you are away for only a couple of days.

Check out the areas in which your cat will be kept to ensure cleanliness and safety.

If you're going to be gone for only a couple of days, you can likely leave your cat at home alone, as long as he has access to a litter box or two, dry food, and water. Don't leave out wet food—if it's not eaten right away, it forms a lovely home for bacteria. If you'll be away for a longer period of time, board your cat or get a pet sitter. It's not fair to your cat to be left unattended for a longer period of time.

Before you make reservations at a kennel, make sure that the cats are kept in a separate area than the dogs. You want your cat to be happy, or at least comfortable, and being kept in the same room with barking dogs is not likely to make your cat happy or comfortable.

Also visit the kennel before you make your reservations. The cages should be in good

shape, with no protruding wires or slivers of wood. The kennel should not smell dirty. Kennels may smell like animals, but they should not smell of urine or feces.

You will need a copy of your cat's vaccination records. Kennel operators want to make sure that all of the cats in their care have the necessary vaccinations and that there's no danger that the cats will either catch or spread diseases.

If your cat has any problems or is on any medication, let the kennel operator know and be sure to supply whatever medicine is needed. If your cat is on a special diet, supply his food. Don't ask for a discount on your boarding bill because you are supplying your own food. You are paying for safe care, and caring for a cat on a special diet adds to the kennel's workload.

Also supply all instructions for your cat's medication and/or special feeding in writing. This way, you don't have to remember everything in the flurry of dropping off your cat, and the kennel staff will have the instructions, even if the same person is not always taking care of your cat. Most kennels will ask for your veterinarian's name and number and for an emergency contact; if they don't ask, offer it anyway.

You may also want to leave instructions that anything out of the ordinary with your cat's health should be treated immediately. I'd rather pay a veterinary bill for something minor than have a minor problem turn into something serious because it was ignored. If I'm going to be away for an extended amount of time, I leave word with my veterinarian that I will pay all bills and that I authorize her to do whatever is necessary in my absence. I don't want the veterinarian to hesitate because she can't reach me or isn't sure what I'd want to do.

Most kennel operators know enough about animals to be able to tell if a cat is sick or hurt. They see their charges many times throughout the day and can pick up on odd behavior that may indicate a problem.

Ask if the kennel does any grooming. You might want your cat to have a bath before he comes home. A bath will catch any fleas that might have found your cat. Good kennels fight fleas and work to keep the premises flea-free, but there's no guarantee that someone else's cat or dog won't bring in some fleas.

Some boarding kennels offer many amenities, giving your cat a mini-vacation of his own.

A pet sitter can give your cat some care
and companionship while you're away.

Some veterinary offices offer boarding, and some owners are very comfortable with that arrangement because there's a veterinarian right there if your cat should become ill. Most veterinary clinics, though, are not specifically set up to care for boarding animals. Sick animals are the priority, and your cat may not get as much attention as you'd like.

Boarding at your vet's clinic makes sense if you have a cat who needs special care each day, such as insulin shots for a diabetic cat. If your veterinarian does offer boarding, get the details on how and where your cat will be kept before you make your decision.

A pet sitter can be a good alternative to boarding, especially if your cat becomes anxious in strange places or if your cat is older and needs more attention than a

kennel can give. An older cat may also get disoriented in a strange place and not adjust well to a kennel, or that older pet may have a bit of arthritis and be uncomfortable in a kennel.

Another benefit to a pet sitter is that it will make your house look like someone is home. There'll be lights on and maybe a car in the driveway at different times. A pet sitter may also be willing to take in the mail, collect newspapers, and water houseplants.

If you live in metropolitan area, you may be able to find a pet sitter through one of these professional organizations: Pet Sitters International (*www.petsit.com*), the National Association of Professional Pet Sitters (*www.petsitters.org*), or Pet Sitters Associates, LLC (*www.petsitllc.com*). You may also find local petsitting companies in your area.

A professional sitter will be bonded and have insurance.

Ask for pet-sitter referrals from your veterinarian's office. Sometimes vet techs also pet-sit, which gives you the added bonus of having someone with medical training taking care of your cat. You might have a friend or neighbor who's willing to help out as well, but don't choose a person just because he or she is convenient. The teen next door may love animals, but is she responsible? Can you trust her to remember your cat's medicine? Will she always remember to clean the litter box? Will she be careful not to let your cat escape if he's an indoor-only cat? A friend or neighbor may recommend a pet sitter, but, even in that case, don't be afraid to ask for references.

Also, what do you want the sitter to do? A sitter who stays overnight at your house will likely charge more than one who just drops by a few times a day. No matter who you hire, be specific in what you expect and put everything in writing. A professional sitter may have a contract, but there may be things you need to add, change, or delete from a basic contract. Don't assume anything. Write out when your cat is to be fed, what type of food you feed, and how much he gets at each meal. Does your cat take any supplements or medications? If your sitter will be eating his or her meals at your house, how do you feel about your cat sharing people food? Make your rules clear.

Post your veterinarian's number, emergency numbers, and numbers where you can be contacted. Tell your veterinarian before you go that the pet sitter has the authority to authorize treatment and that you will pay all bills.

Importantly, your sitter needs to come to your home and meet your cat before you go away. Depending on your cat, you may want to have the sitter come more than once, and it might be a good idea for the sitter to visit once when you're not home to see how your cat reacts when you're not there to make introductions. Make sure the sitter and your cat are comfortable with each other. You are depending on that person to take care of your cat in your absence.

Once you've chosen either a boarding facility or a pet sitter, harden your heart as you leave your cat behind. Enjoy your vacation, knowing that your pet will be well cared for.

The first step in traveling with your cat is helping him feel comfortable in his carrier.

While you may never travel across the country with your cat, you will at least need to make some trips by car, even if it's just to the veterinarian or groomer. A cat may seem to hate car travel, but it could be that he dislikes the carrier. Take time to get your cat used to a carrier. If the car still seems to be a problem, work on conditioning your cat to the car. Every day, put your cat in his carrier and put the carrier in the car. Feed him tasty treats while he's in the car and then take the cat back into the house. Keep these sessions short and happy.

Eventually, you'll work up to starting the engine and then to driving the length of the driveway. If you've got a helper, have that person give the cat treats to help to take his mind off the road. Do this every day until your cat seems comfortable and then start increasing the length of your trips from around the block to around town.

Even if your cat loves car rides, never travel with your cat loose in the car. A loose cat in a car can be a real danger, especially if he interferes with the driver or gets under the pedals. If there's an accident, a loose cat is likely to end up going through the windshield. If a cat manages to be unhurt in an accident, he may escape the car and be lost or injured. The best way for your cat to travel is in a carrier, with the carrier on the floor against the front seat. The next best position is in a carrier that is securely fastened to the seat. A good choice, but not the best, is to secure your cat with a harness that attaches to the car's seat-belt system.

It's hard to leave your cat behind when you're on vacation, and, while many cats find it stressful to be in new environments and are happier at home, people do travel with their cats. It's a little extra work, but it's nice to have your cat with you.

When traveling with your cat, carry water from home. If you're going to be gone for an extended period, gradually add water from your destination to the water you've brought with you so that there's not a sudden change. Travel with enough of your cat's usual food, too. A food that's common in your store at home may not be so common at your destination. Travel can be stressful for your

cat, so try to keep as many things constant as possible. If you cook for your cat or feed raw, you'll need a good cooler so that the food doesn't spoil.

Carry food and water dishes for your cat, or you can carry just a water bowl and serve the cat's food on disposable paper plates. This can be convenient if you're feeding a meal on the road or are camping.

If your cat is on any medication, make sure you have enough with you for the entire trip. Carry your cat's vaccination record with you as well, especially if you are traveling across state lines or into another country. A small first-aid kit is a good idea, too.

You'll need to bring some kind of litter box. Depending on the length of your trip, you may be able to use something as simple as a cardboard box that you can throw away at your destination. Many people find a roasting pan a good size for travel. Carry enough of your cat's preferred litter, too. In the middle of a trip is not the best time for your cat to decide he won't use the strange litter.

As you travel, you may be planning to stop at tourist attractions along the way. Consider your cat before you make those stops. Some attractions have boarding facilities, but many do not, and many may only accommodate dogs. Do you plan to leave your cat in the car? A cat in a car in the summer is not a good idea. Even with the

windows down, the interior temperature of a car can reach lethal temperatures. Parking in the shade is no guarantee that your cat will be safe, either. As the sun moves, so does the shade, and your car could end up with no shade at all. Never leave your cat unattended in a car in the summer. A cat's cooling system is not very efficient, and stress decreases that efficiency. It doesn't take long for a cat to overheat and die. If you can't leave your cat in your hotel room or at a boarding facility, skip the attraction.

Another thing to think about if you're taking your cat with you on vacation is where you'll be staying.

Travel with a first-aid kit in case of a mishap on the road.

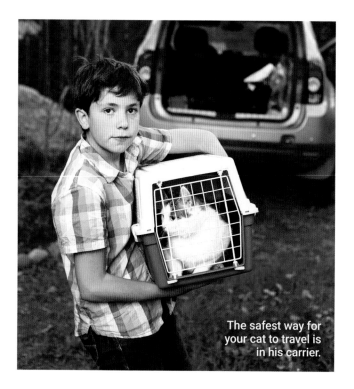

The safest way for your cat to travel is in his carrier.

called *Traveling with Your Pet*, which is a great starting place, but because many are geared toward dogs, always call and confirm that cats are welcome. Also, find out ahead of time if the motel charges extra for cats. Some places have a one-time pet fee, while some charge for each night. These fees may be reasonable, or you may find that it's cheaper to leave your cat at home with a pet sitter or in a boarding kennel.

The same rules apply for camping. Make sure that the campground allows cats; if it does, find out the rules before you arrive. State and federal camping areas will require proof that your cat has been vaccinated against rabies, so don't forget that paperwork.

Even if you're staying with friends or relatives, make sure they know ahead of time that you'll be bringing your cat. Even if they know and like your cat, they may not be prepared to have the cat in their home. Think about what your destination is like. Are there other cats? Are there children? If your cat has grown up with children, he'll likely be fine, but if a cat isn't used to children, they can make him nervous and uncomfortable.

If you're staying at a motel, or if you'll be staying at different motels as you travel, make sure your cat is welcome before you check in. AAA offers members a book of pet-friendly motels, hotels, and campgrounds

If you're staying in a motel room, never leave your cat loose when you're not there. Put him in his carrier when you're not in the room with him. When you leave, turn on a radio or television so that the noise masks outside noises that might upset your cat.

At home, your cat may be able to lounge on your bed all the time, but at a motel, housekeeping won't appreciate cat hair all over the bedspread. Travel with a couple of sheets so that you can cover the bed with them. Carry a piece of plastic to put under food and water dishes to catch any spills and another piece for under the litter box.

If you think housekeeping will bother your cat, hang out the "do not disturb" sign. You can make your own bed, and, if you want clean towels, you can always make arrangements to put the dirty ones outside the door, where housekeeping can leave you clean ones.

If possible, try to stay in rooms that open onto an inside corridor rather than to the outdoors. Then, if your cat ever gets out the door, he's still in a contained area, not in a parking lot or on a busy road.

If you enjoy traveling by bus, you're out of luck if you want your cat with you. Greyhound buses allow service animals only. If you prefer a train, Amtrak has begun allowing small cats and dogs for a fee. Local trains and buses may have their own rules, so check first before you risk being turned away.

Flying may be another method of transportation to consider. If you have a small cat, you may be able to put him in an under-the-seat carrier, but many airlines limit the number of pets allowed on a flight, so don't assume you can take your cat on board. Check with the airline first. Many people fly with their cats with no problems, but you do need to be aware of all regulations, which vary from airline to airline. You can't just show up at the airport with your cat in a carrier.

Be considerate hotel guests when traveling with your pets.

61 Losing Your Cat

No one wants to think of his or her pet as lost, but sometimes it happens. Following these guidelines can help get your cat returned to you. In addition to these suggestions, search carefully around your house. If your cat is frightened, he may be under your porch or behind the bushes next to your house. If there's a shed or a garage nearby, look there, too. Look up. Your cat may be crouched on a rafter or on top of a cupboard.

No matter what kind of identification you use for your cat, don't rely solely on a tag or a microchip to get your cat back should he become lost. With luck, your cat will never go missing, but if it does happen, don't waste time—be proactive in working to get your cat home.

Make posters and flyers. Include a photo of your cat, and make sure that the picture is clear, with the cat against a contrasting background. Your cat may look adorable in a pile of pillows, but can a stranger tell what your cat really looks like from that picture? Besides the photo, include your phone number, the general area where your cat was lost, and your cat's sex and age. It may be more helpful to say "kitten" or "older cat with gray muzzle" than to give his exact age.

A lost cat might not be easy to spot outdoors.

TRUE COLORS

If the only photo you have of your cat is in black and white, describe your cat's color. Use terms that everyone will understand. Instead of saying "calico" say "black, brown, and white."

Offer a reward, but don't specify the amount on the poster.

Once you've got posters and flyers made, go door-to-door to hand out flyers and ask your neighbors to keep an eye out for your cat. Put posters on area bulletin boards and at veterinarian's offices.

Recruit children to help. Children are likely to cover more territory on foot than adults, and they may be more likely to notice a cat. Don't encourage children to try to catch your cat. Ask them to come to you or to tell their parents to call you. A lost cat is frequently a frightened cat, and you don't want him to be chased farther away or to bite or claw someone out of fear.

Call area veterinarians. Maybe your cat was hit by a car and taken to an animal hospital. Check the local shelter. Go in person. Don't rely on phone calls, and don't rely on having someone at a shelter call you. Leave your name and phone number, of course, but also check in person. Notes can be lost, and shelter personnel may change. As clearly as you may describe your cat, the person listening may be picturing a different look entirely. A fluffy white cat can mean many things to different people, as can words like "small," "medium," and "large." Even if you mention a specific breed, a person may not be familiar with that breed. Or you may have a mixed breed that doesn't really look like a specific breed. Coat length and color will be more descriptive than the breed's name.

Go look at the cats that have been picked up as strays. Look at least every other day. Show the staff pictures of your cat and leave a photo for the next shift. If there's another shelter in the vicinity, visit it, too. It's possible that someone could pick up your cat and then either release him farther away or lose him again.

Run an ad in the lost and found column of the newspaper and ask local radio stations to announce it. Many times these announcements are free in both newspapers and on the radio. Make sure you read the ads placed in the "found" column.

Use social media. Many rescue organizations post cats they've found on Facebook, and sometimes people who've found a cat will also post. Post your lost pet and keep checking to see if anyone reports seeing your cat. A friend of mine had a cat who was missing for over two weeks. Finally, the local shelter posted the cat's picture on Facebook, and my friend was reunited with his cat.

Don't give up too soon. Someone may be feeding a "stray" or may have taken your cat in and not yet seen an ad or a poster. I hope you never need this information, but, if you do, it may help you get your cat home safe and sound.

No matter where you live, there's always a chance that you'll face an emergency situation someday. It could be a hurricane, a house fire, or a blizzard that leaves you homeless and in need of shelter elsewhere. With a little advance planning, you can increase the odds that your feline friend will survive an emergency situation safe and sound.

Sometimes, if the danger is immediate, we need to make the heartbreaking decision to leave home without our pets. For many emergency situations, though, you'll have enough warning to make a few preparations, including gathering up the family cat. So, have a carrier for each of your pets, and keep those carriers in an easy-to-reach location,

such as by your door or in the garage. Your cat's carrier should be ready to go. Your carrier isn't going to do you much good in an emergency if you can't get to it or it isn't put together.

Keep a sturdy pillowcase or a strong mesh laundry bag to contain your cat if you can't get to your pet carrier. The bag will fold up and won't take up much space, so you can even leave it in your car. Keep a pair of heavy gloves with those bags. No matter how calm or loving your cat may be, all bets are off in an emergency. You cat will be as tense as you are, and an anxious, frightened cat may decide it's time to use his claws.

Think about where your cat will hide. Cats tend to seek out the lowest, darkest, most hidden spaces they can find when they're frightened. Pay attention to where your cat goes when he hides. For instance, your cat may head for the basement, where there may be many hiding places. If you have a large, cluttered basement, and your cat is likely to go under a workbench and behind several boxes, it may be time to make the basement off limits to your cat. In an emergency, you're not going to have time to search all of the wonderful hidey-holes in your basement.

If your cat typically hides in a closet, that's probably OK. Most closets are small enough to make it possible for you to snare your cat. If your cat likes hiding under the bed, keep a yardstick or a broom handle near the bed to get the cat out. Or, if you have the strength, just flip the mattress and springs of the bed.

Have a cat carrier ready to go in case of emergency.

Don't forget that many cats like to hide in the box springs. If that's your cat's favorite hideout, and you have advance notice of an emergency situation, such as an impending hurricane, seal up the hole.

A frightened cat will find a dark, remote place to hide.

If you don't think you can retrieve a frightened cat from under a bed, consider setting springs and bed directly on the floor, so there's no space at all underneath. Or, you can fill the space with storage boxes or surround the open area with wooden slats that will block the space.

Many cats don't wear collars, but consider getting a collar and ID tags for your cat, as well as getting your cat microchipped, so that if your cat ends up running loose in an emergency situation, whoever finds him will be able to get him back to you safely. If your cat is used to wearing a harness and being on a leash, that's another plus, especially if you end up in a shelter. You can use the harness and leash to allow your cat a bit of freedom from his carrier while still keeping him under control.

Keep a copy of your cat's vaccination records in your glove compartment or with your own important documents in case you need to evacuate. If you live somewhere where an emergency situation is likely, keep any medications your cat may need with the carrier. Rotate monthly so it's always fresh. Keep a large jug of water in the car and replace it periodically. Know how much food your cat will need if you'll be away from home for an extended period of time and keep that much on hand. Keep a small litter box and some litter with your other emergency supplies. Another bag might include paper towels and a box of premoistened baby wipes for clean up and a small bottle of cleaner for sanitizing, as well as some towels for bedding.

If it happens that you have no choice but to leave your cat behind, leave the doors or some windows open so that your cat can escape. You may never be reunited, but your cat will have a better chance of survival than if he is shut up in the house.

PART XI

Just for Fun

Years ago, I always thought of wild cats as large cats, like lions and tigers, snow leopards, cheetahs, cougars, and even lynx and bobcats, but I am fascinated by all of the smaller wild cats that exist, many of which are the size of the domestic cats that share our homes. All of the cats described here weigh less than 20 pounds (9.1 kg), and most weigh less than 10 pounds (4.5 kg). Many are endangered or likely may soon be. With a little imagination, any of these cats could be sharing our homes.

African Wildcat

The African Wildcat, the cat behind all of our domestic cats, is also known as the Near Eastern Wildcat. This cat lives in North Africa, in the Near East, and around the edge of the Arabian Peninsula. It has sandy gray fur with a dark dorsal stripe, pale vertical stripes on the sides, and, like the Sand Cat (described later), two dark rings on the forelegs. These small carnivores weigh between 7 and 10 pounds (3.2–4.5 kg).

Bay Cat

The Bay Cat, sometimes called the Bornean Bay Cat or just the Bornean Cat, lives on the island of Borneo. This cat has a gorgeous chestnut red coat and weighs between 6 and 9 pounds (2.7–4.1 kg). They are very rare and considered endangered by the International Union for Conservation of Nature (IUCN).

A modern-day African Wildcat in South Africa.

Black-Footed Cat

The Black-Footed Cat, sometimes called the Small-Spotted Cat, is a native of the desert areas of Southern Africa and is listed as vulnerable by the IUCN. This cat's head, face, and ears look very much like those of a cat who could be curled up on a bed and pampered as a house pet. It has a reddish coat, patterned with dark spots that form rings on the legs, neck, and tail, and weighs between 3 and 6 pounds (1.4–2.7 kg).

Flat-Headed Cat

The Flat-Headed Cat got its name from its head, which is long and narrow and has a flattened forehead. The cat is found only in

The Black-Footed Cat is among the smallest found in Africa.

Borneo, Sumatra, and Peninsular Malaysia and is listed as endangered. The breed weighs in between 3 and 6 pounds (1.4–2.7 kg) and lives mainly on aquatic prey. It has short legs and a short tail and is covered with reddish brown to dark brown fur. Its claws are semiretractable.

Geoffroy's Cat

Geoffroy's Cat is found in the southern and central regions of South America and is a good swimmer, enjoying aquatic prey as well as small mammals and birds. In the northern area of its range, the breed's fur is brownish yellow with black spots as well as dark bands on the legs, tail, head, and neck. Further south, the fur tends to be grayer, but still with black spots and bands. Some cats may be solid black. A Geoffroy's typically weighs between 4 and 11 pounds (1.8–5.0 kg), but some may reach up to 17 pounds (7.7 kg).

Iriomote

The Iriomote is found only on the Japanese island of Iriomote and is critically endangered, with a declining population of fewer than three hundred. These cats have thick, muscular necks and shoulders but are fairly weak jumpers. They eat a wide variety of prey and are especially good at catching aquatic animals. They are dark brown, marked with darker spots that merge into bands. Each ear has a white central spot on the back, like a tiger's. They weigh between 6 and 11 pounds (2.7–5.0 kg).

Jaguarundi

The Jaguarundi, also known as the Eyra Cat, weighs between 6 and 15 pounds (2.7–6.8 kg). These lovely cats come in black, chestnut red, or a brownish gray and range from southern Texas through Argentina. They have long, slender bodies; long tails; and short legs. They hunt mainly on the ground and are not endangered.

Geoffroy's Cat, *Felis geoffroyi*.

The Jaguarundi, or Eyra Cat, can be found in the southern United States and South America.

Kodkod

The Kodkod, or Guigna, is another South American cat, living mainly in central and southern Chile and into Argentina. It is similar in appearance to Geoffroy's Cat but is smaller and has a thicker tail. The breed weighs between 4 and 6 pounds (1.8–2.7 kg) and is listed by the IUCN as vulnerable.

Margay

The Margay is another small wildcat, weighing between 5 and 9 pounds (2.3–4.1 kg), and found in Central and South America as well as in southern Mexico. Its markings are similar to those of the Ocelot, and the breed is sometimes called the "Tree Ocelot" because of this similarity and the fact that these cats spend almost their entire lives in the trees, although they do sometimes hunt on the ground. The female Margay has only two teats and gives birth to one kitten, but sometimes, not often, two. The breed is listed as near threatened by the IUCN.

Pallas's Cat

Pallas's Cat lives in Central Asia and Eurasia and is ideally suited for life in cold, arid regions with its long, thick coat and particularly long hair on the stomach. This endangered cat weighs between 5 and 9 pounds (2.3–4.1 kg) but looks larger because of all of its fur. Because its ears are on the sides of the head instead of on top, the Pallas's Cat looks permanently cranky, which it may be.

These cats live solitary lives in rocky habitat. They are hunted for their fur and for their fat and organs, which are used to make folk medicines. The IUCN classifies the Pallas's Cat as near threatened, which means it is expected to be an endangered species soon.

A Margay in the Panamanian rain forest.

Rusty-Spotted Cat

The Rusty-Spotted Cat is listed by the ICUN as near threatened in its habitat of India, Nepal, and Sri Lanka. This little cat weighs between 2 and 4 pounds (0.9–1.8 kg) and is gray with rust-colored spots.

Sand Cat

Sand Cats are small cats weighing between 3 and 8 pounds (1.4–3.6 kg) who live in the deserts of Africa, the Middle East, and Central Asia. While they are definitely wild, they look like sweet little sand-colored cats who'd be right at home as family companions. The Sand Cat has dark bars on its legs, and the tail has a black tip with black rings. The rest of the coat may be solid or may have spots and/or stripes. The well-furred feet make the cat's tracks almost invisible. Because its habitat is the desert, the Sand Cat rarely ever drinks water, living on the moisture from its prey.

Scottish Wildcat

With Scottish ancestors, I have a soft spot for the Scottish Wildcat, a cat that is practically extinct in the wild, with only several hundred believed to be alive. These cats range in size, depending on gender, from 5 pounds to 16 pounds (2.3–7.3 kg). They might be mistaken for domestic tabby cats, but their tails are thicker and blunt-ended, and there's no dorsal stripe. Their heads are also larger. Because they look so much like a domestic cat, they are frequently shot.

Southern Tiger Cat

The Southern Tiger Cat, also known as the Southern Little Spotted Cat, is a small South American cat listed as vulnerable by the IUCN. These cats are long, sleek, and spotted like leopards but weigh only between 3 and 7 pounds (1.4–3.2 kg).

The Sand Cat, *Felis margarita*.

A polydactyl orange tabby cat.

Most cats have just eighteen toes: four on each back foot and five on each front foot. *Polydactyls* (Greek for "many fingers") are cats with extra toes. The extra toes are usually on the front feet, but sometimes a cat will have extra toes on both the front and the back feet. You will never find a polydactyl with extra toes on just the back feet. Poyldactyls are more prevalent on the east coast of North America and on the west coast of the British Isles.

Almost everyone has heard of the cats owned by writer Ernest Hemingway. A sea captain gave Hemingway his first polydactyl, a cat named Snow White. This cat had kittens, and many had the extra toes of their mother. Today, the Ernest Hemingway Home and Museum in Key West, Florida, is home to about forty polydactyl cats.

Polydactyl cats were considered good luck by sailors and, because of their many toes, the sailors thought that they could maintain their balance easier on a moving deck than regular cats. They also thought that the extra toes made these cats more efficient hunters, so it was common to find groups of polydactyl cats in port cities. The name "Cardi cats" derives from the port of Cardigan (*Aberteifi* in Welsh), which was once one of the busiest seaports in Wales.

When the dewclaw is larger, the cat may earn the nickname "mitten cat" or "thumb cat." The cat may have a duplicate dewclaw; the extra toes may form a wide foot, called a "patty foot"; or extra, undeveloped toes may be located between the regular toes. The Guinness World Record holder for the most toes was a cat called Jake, who had twenty-eight toes, but The Messy Beast (*www.messybeast.com*) states that the record number of toes is thirty-two, held by a cat named Mickey Mouse who had eight toes on each paw.

Most polydactyl cats have no trouble at all with their extra toes, and the toes may help the cat grasp things more easily; in some cases, the cat can even open drawers or doors. Sometimes the toes grow in such a way as to cause embedded nails, or, if the toes curl under, the nails may grow into the pads of the feet. There might be a greater risk of the cat catching a nail on carpeting, but keeping his nails trimmed should eliminate any problems.

The polydactyl gene is likely an incomplete dominant, which means that a cat with extra toes may be heterozygous or homozygous. In cats with only the polydactyl gene, there is a possibility that the cat may have a condition called radial hypoplasia, or "twisty cat" syndrome, in which the front legs are shorter and malformed. This is more likely in cats with "patty" paws than in those with "mitten" or "thumb" paws. Cats with radial hypoplasia are sometimes called "squittens" or "kangaroo cats" because their front legs are so short that they look a bit like squirrels or kangaroos when they sit on their haunches.

If a cat has dewclaws, he is likely heterozygous and will not have radial hypoplasia. Polydactyl cats without dewclaws cannot be shown, but they may produce normal-footed cats as long as they are bred to nonpolydactyl cats.

NICKNAMES
Polydactyl cats are sometimes called "gypsy cats," "mitten cats," "thumb cats," "six-finger cats," "boxing cats," "Cardi cats," and "Hemingway cats."

A polydactyl Maine Coon Cat.

Is the US Capitol haunted by a ghost cat?

Some cats are known by the company they keep, and some become famous—or notorious—in their own right. An example is the Demon Cat, a ghost cat who haunts the Capitol building in Washington, DC. Some say the ghost was the mother of a litter disturbed during the construction of the building; others say it's the ghost of the last cat in a colony of cats brought in to eliminate the rat population. The Demon Cat is seen prior to national disasters, such as assassinations of public figures or stock-market crashes.

Stubbs the cat was a write-in candidate for mayor of Talkeetna, Alaska, when voters decided they didn't like any of the humans who were running. Stubbs served as mayor for almost twenty years.

Winston Churchill loved cats, and one of his favorites was an orange cat named Jock, who lived with him at his home, Chartwell. Churchill's will stipulated that an orange cat should be kept at Chartwell forever as a tribute to Jock.

RICH CAT
Tommasco became a famous cat when he inherited ten million dollars upon his owner's death.

Abraham Lincoln brought a cat named Tabby with him to the White House, and he adopted another cat, named Dixie. He is famously quoted as saying that Dixie was more clever than his entire cabinet.

INTERNET FAMOUS

The Internet has made several cats, including Grumpy Cat, famous for their antics.

You can learn more about many different pets owned by various presidents at the Presidential Pet Museum site (*www.presidentialpetmuseum.com*), but here are a few others who had cats.

Siamese cats made an appearance in the United States in 1879 when the American consul in Bangkok gave a cat named Siam to President Rutherford B. Hayes and his wife, Lucy. Gerald Ford's daughter Susan had a Siamese named Shan, and Amy Carter had a Siamese named Misty Malarky Ying Yang.

Calvin Coolidge had Tiger, a tabby cat, and many people remember Socks, the companion of the Clinton family. George and Laura Bush had a black cat named India. Tom Kitten, also known as Tom Terrific, belonged to Caroline Kennedy. Because of President Kennedy's allergy to cats, Tom Kitten lived most of his short life with a staff member. According to the Presidential Pet Museum, an original photograph of the cat sold for $14,950 in 1996.

DID YOU KNOW?

Facebook is Grumpy Cat's primary source of attention with close to 9 million likes!

A 1995 US postage stamp to honor the Krazy Kat comic strip.

I love cartoon cats, and apparently I'm not the only one. Wikipedia lists 124 cartoon cats! So, even though knowing about them is not essential to owning a cat, they offer a smile and may even mirror your cat's behavior.

One of the earliest newspaper cartoons to feature a cat was *Krazy Kat*, drawn by George Herriman. The strip ran from 1913 to 1944 and featured Krazy Kat, a black cat referred to as both "he" and "she" in the strip, and Ignatz, a white mouse whom Krazy Kat loved. While not wildly popular at the time, this comic strip inspired many modern cartoonists.

Kliban cats, drawn by Bernard Kliban, first appeared in *Playboy* magazine in the early 1970s, and Kliban published his first book of cats in 1975. The typical Kliban cat is a large "meatloaf" cat, and, while Kliban died in 1990, you can still buy merchandise featuring the pudgy gray and black tabby.

Heathcliff, by George Gately (now written and drawn by Gately's nephew, Peter Gallagher), first appeared in 1973 and is distributed by Creators Syndicate. It's a single-panel cartoon, except on Sundays, when this wily cat gets a full Sunday strip to make mischief. "Kitty Korner," a part of Heathcliff's Sunday strip, features real cats who do unusual things.

Heathcliff, like the famous cartoon cat Garfield, is an orange cat with black stripes, but he's much more active than Garfield. Garfield is rarely seen away from home, but Heathcliff roams the neighborhood, exploring garbage cans, swiping fish from the fish market, and frequently enjoying the attention of a bevy of admiring girlfriends.

My favorite cartoon is still *Calvin and Hobbes*, by Bill Watterson. This cartoon featured a small boy, Calvin, and his stuffed tiger, Hobbes, and ran from 1985 to 1995, distributed by Universal Press Syndicate.

Hobbes is Calvin's best friend, but that doesn't mean he always follows Calvin into trouble. Like any self-respecting cat, Hobbes will occasionally sneak off and take a nap before the fire, leaving Calvin to toboggan down a dangerous hill by himself. Hobbes likes girls, especially girls with green eyes and "whiskers…long whiskers." He's fond of tuna, but he's not above reminding Calvin that he will consider other protein sources, such as Calvin himself. I think house cats sometimes feel the same way.

Garfield, by Jim Davis, has been around since 1978 and currently holds the Guinness World Record as the world's most widely syndicated comic strip; it is distributed by Universal Press Syndicate. Garfield likes creature comforts—lots of food and frequent naps—and who can argue with that? Lasagna and a nap always sound good to me.

Garfield also has his own website, which, if you're a Garfield fan, is the place to shop for all things Garfield.

Bucky is the creation of Darby Conley and has appeared in the daily strip *Get Fuzzy* since 1999. Bucky is an always-cranky Siamese. His ears are always plastered back, and, judging from his expression, I'd keep my distance and think twice about extending a hand and saying, "Nice kitty."

The total opposite of Bucky is Carlyle in the cartoon *Kit 'n' Carlyle* by Larry Wright. Carlyle, an adorable little black kitten with a white face and paws, has been around

since 1980. He loves soft places for naps and enjoys playing in paper bags. He's not as food-motivated as Hobbes, Garfield, or Heathcliff, but maybe that's because he's not fond of his owner's cooking. Carlyle can outstare any of Kit's boyfriends, which may be why she's still single.

The 1998 US postage stamp featuring the delightful duo of Sylvester and Tweety.

Some cats don't get their own comic strip but have guest appearances in other cartoons. Siamese cat King Tut sometimes shares the spotlight with the cartoon Great Dane Marmaduke, and two very different cats sometimes joined the Peanuts gang, created by Charles Schulz. My favorite is Faron, generally shown draped over Frieda's arms, and obviously a Ragdoll, although the breed is never mentioned. The other cat, referred to as "the cat next door," is never shown, but he terrorizes Snoopy and frequently shreds Snoopy's doghouse with razor-sharp claws.

Bill the Cat was created in the 1980s by Berkeley Breathed. This homely-looking orange tiger cat, purportedly the illegitimate son of Garfield, was probably best known for hacking up large hairballs with the

A 2014 Swiss postage stamp honored Garfield and his legendary appetite.

corresponding sound of "ack!" Bill the Cat can still be seen on Facebook.

One of the earliest animated cats was Felix, a cartoon cat who first appeared in 1919. Accounts differ as to whether Otto Messmer or Pat Sullivan created Felix, but Felix was popular until about 1932. Joe Oriolo resurrected him as a television cartoon in 1953, and, in 2002, *TV Guide* ranked Felix the Cat as number twenty-eight on a list of the fifty greatest cartoon characters. If you've ever seen a wall clock shaped like a cat with moving eyes and a swinging tail, it is based on Felix.

Tom, the cat of the *Tom and Jerry* cartoons, was the next animated cat to arrive on the scene. William Hanna and Joseph Barbera created Tom along with Jerry the mouse in 1940. Tom and Jerry's adventures were so popular that they got their own full-length movie in 1992. Although you won't see them in movie theaters anymore, they are featured in several direct-to-video films and are popular on YouTube.

Sylvester the cat (full name Sylvester J. Pussycat, Sr.) first appeared in 1945, and he teamed up with Tweety Bird in 1947. Together, the lisping "puddy tat" and the clever canary delighted audiences until 1964. Sylvester continued on his own until 1966. In 1998, the cartoon duo was honored with a United States postage stamp.

Fritz the Cat was a college-student cat created by Robert Crumb. Fritz was on the scene as a comic strip between 1965 and 1972 and in the movie *Fritz the Cat*, written and directed by Ralph Bakshi, in 1972. This film has the distinction of being the first X-rated animated film.

We're more used to movies like *The Aristocats*, a 1970 Walt Disney movie about a kidnapped cat, her three kittens, and the alley cat who helps them get home. Go back to 1955, when the classic *Lady and the Tramp* was released with the two mischievous Siamese cats, Si and Am, voiced by Peggy Lee.

Memorabilia from *Tom and Jerry* shows the famous pair in action.

67 Cat Books

These books are my personal favorites. There are a lot more out there in every category, but these should give you a good start. Check out the Cat Writers' Assocation's website (*www.catwriters.com*) for a list of more authors and their books.

Nonfiction

Cat Scene Investigator by Dusty Rainbolt. This book is a must if you eventually have multiple cats.

Memoirs

Amber, A Very Personal Cat by Gladys Taber. The author shares anecdotes about life with her Abyssinian as well as cat-care advice.

Conversations with Amber by Gladys Taber. The author chronicles her relationship with her remarkable cat, Amber.

The Fur Person by May Sarton. A classic based on the life and adventures of the author's cat.

For Fun

Cats into Everything and *The Cats' House* by Bob Walker. Walker and his wife, Frances Mooney, share their amazing house, decorated especially to keep their multiple cats happy, in these two fun books.

Ghost Cats: Human Encounters with Feline Spirits by Dusty Rainbolt with illustrations by Stephanie Piro. This is an illustrated collection of anecdotes describing eerie encounters with felines.

Funky Cats Coloring Book by Brenda Abdoyan. Relax and be creative with old-school coloring fun.

Dean Russo Tilted Head Cat Journal. Hardcover lined journal featuring cover art by Dean Russo. There's a whole line of these cat- and dog-themed journals.

My Cat's Album is a scrapbook for all cat lovers. So cute!

Boredom Busters for Cats by Nikki Moustaki. Give your cat some fun mental and physical stimulation.

Novels

The Cat Who… mysteries by Lillian Jackson Braun. Two Siamese cats feature in these books.

The Joe Grey series by Shirley Rousseau Murphy. These light murder mysteries feature Joe Grey, a cat who can communicate with his owner.

The Midnight Louis series by Carole Nelson Douglas. A black cat helps solve mysteries in Las Vegas.

Multiple mystery series featuring cats by Clea Simon.

Training

Clicker Training for Cats by Karen Pryor. A beginner's guide to this positive-training technique geared toward the cat owner.

Naughty No More by Marilyn Krieger. Advice on using reward-based training methods, such as clicker training, to eliminate problem behaviors.

wanted to include many more cat jokes, but too many played off the word "cat" or "purr." For example, what kind of comb do you use to groom a cat? A catacomb. Or, how is cat food generally sold? Purr can. So, I decided to go for quality rather than quantity. Here are five jokes that, if they didn't make me laugh out loud, at least made me smile. They're not purrfect, but they're not catastrophic either.

WHERE DOES A CAT GO WHEN HE LOSES HIS TAIL?

A retail store.

WHY IS IT SO HARD FOR A LEOPARD TO HIDE?

Because he's always spotted.

WHAT DO YOU GET WHEN YOU CROSS A CHICK WITH A CAT?

A peeping Tom.

WHY DID THE CAT RUN FROM THE TREE?

He was afraid of the bark.

WHY DON'T CATS PLAY POKER?

Too many cheetahs.

The story goes that after Muezza, Mohammed's cat, saved him from a venomous snake, Mohammed granted all cats the ability to always land on their feet. Wherever it came from, cats do have what is called a "righting reflex." Because of his very flexible backbone and lack of a collarbone, a cat can successfully twist his body so that he always lands on all fours. While falling, a cat will spread his legs, increasing his drag and lowering his terminal velocity. Cats are more apt to die when falling from heights lower than six stories because they haven't yet relaxed and spread their bodies. However, while a cat may survive a fall from a great height, he may still sustain serious injuries that require medical treatment for the cat to survive.

Cats have mobile ears that can move independently of each other.

Female cats are more likely to be right-handed. Researchers at Queen's University in Belfast collected data on which paw cats used when stepping down stairs or over objects and what paw they used when reaching for food. In all cases, males tended to use their left paws, while females were more likely to use their right paws.

Cats have thirty-two muscles that control each ear. Humans have six ear muscles.

Cats are known for their flexibility and agility.

DID YOU KNOW?
The oldest cat ever is Crème Puff, who was born on August 3, 1967 and lived until August 6, 2005— an amazing **38 years and 3 days!**

In the wild, kittens are taught to hunt by their mothers. Domestic cats often fail to learn how to hunt. If a domestic cat catches something, he may bring it to you to kill because he doesn't know how.

Oscar the cat, who lives at the Steere Nursing and Rehabilitation Center in Providence, Rhode Island, curls up for naps next to patients, but only if they're about to die. He's not very friendly to those who are healthy, but he's there to comfort those who are dying. When doctors or nurses notice Oscar's behavior, they call the patient's family and urge them to come and say good-bye.

Color between the shoulder blades, as displayed by this Turkish Van, is considered good luck.

Although there are other claims on the Internet, *Guinness World Records* lists the loudest purr ever recorded at 67.7 decibels, by a British cat named Smokey. In comparison, the Occupational Safety and Health Administration (OSHA) standards list 90 decibels as the level of a lawn mower and 95 decibels as the level of a motorcycle or a chainsaw.

Many Turkish Vans have a small mark between their shoulder blades that fanciers call the "thumbprint of God" or "mark of Allah." It's believed to be good luck.

All Siamese cats are born white.

Ever since cats rid Venice of rats several hundred years ago, the Italian city has held cats in high esteem and has bestowed citizenship on them.

According to *Guinness World Records*, the cat with the longest tail was a female silver Maine Coon named Cygnus, whose tail measured 17.58 inches long. A cat named Arcturus, who lived with the same family as Cygnus, was the tallest domestic cat, with a height of 19.05 inches. He weighed 30 pounds (13.6 kg). Unfortunately, both cats were killed in a house fire in late 2017.

A newborn Siamese
kitten is all white.

Theodore Roosevelt had a polydactyl cat named Slippers.

Cats spend sixteen hours a day sleeping.

Cats spend 30 percent of their waking time grooming themselves.

Many cat owners—95 percent of them, to be exact—admit that they talk to their cats. I think that the other 5 percent are lying.

A running cat can reach a speed of twenty-five miles per hour.

St. Gertrude is the patron saint of cats.

70 Myths and Legends

I love myths and stories of all kinds, and here are a few relating to cats.

Breeders have pretty much bred out both the kink tails and the crossed eyes from Siamese cats, but the stories remain of how the breed originally acquired these traits. One version has it that a king was slowly becoming weaker and weaker. The royal physicians determined that his wine was being poisoned, but no one could tell how. His loyal cat began sleeping with his tail wrapped tightly around the king's cup, so that anyone touching the cup would awaken the cat. While the poisoner was never caught, neither was he able to complete the job of killing the king, and from that day forward, all Siamese cats have had kinks in their tails.

Another version has a pair of Siamese cats finding a sacred golden goblet. The male cat ran off to alert the priests while the female

The kinked tail is not seen often in Siamese cats today.

stayed to guard the goblet, wrapping her tail around its stem. By the time the male returned with the priests, the female had a permanent kink in her tail, a trait she passed on to her kittens. In a similar version, the female not only wrapped her tail around the goblet but also didn't want to let it out of her sight. She stared fixedly at the goblet, developing crossed eyes because of staring so closely and intently for so long.

Another story tells of a beautiful princess who decided to go swimming in a lake, so she placed her rings on the tail of her cat for safekeeping. The rings kept sliding on the tail, and the cat was afraid he would lose the rings until he realized that he could bend the tip of his tail to keep the rings in place. The weather was warm and the water was cool, so the princess spent all afternoon in the water. By the time she returned to the cat, his tail had acquired a permanent kink.

Siamese cats can have a genetic tendency toward crossed eyes.

In the book *Sagwa, the Chinese Siamese Cat*, written in 1994 by Amy Tan and illustrated by Gretchen Schields, a beautiful "pearl white" cat found herself on a magistrate's desk, where she tipped over a bottle of ink. She got it on her face and tried to scrub it off with her paws, meanwhile getting more and more ink on the magistrate's paperwork. Unfortunately, the ink was permanent, and the pearl white cat now had a black tail, black face, and black paws.

The distinctive "M" on the forehead of tabby cats has led to at least two legends. In one version, a tabby cat jumped up into the manger and curled up next to the baby Jesus to keep him warm. Mary marked the cat with an "M" as a sign of her thanks. In another version, the prophet Mohammed decided to cut off the sleeve of his robe rather than disturb his cat, who was curled up on it, asleep. Thereafter, all tabbies were born with an "M" on their forehead as a sign of Mohammed's love for all cats.

The tabby's coloration includes a distinctive "M" on the head.

Pussy willow buds are reminiscent of little gray kittens.

According to a Polish legend, a mother cat once stood on the banks of a river, crying because her kittens had fallen in and were drowning. The willows along the bank dipped their long branches into the water, and the kittens grabbed on and were brought to shore. In memory of that day, each spring, willow branches sprout fur-like buds at their tips where the kittens once clung.

In another version, a flood hit a city, and the cats fled to the mountains. The kittens couldn't run as fast as the adults, and when they reached a row of willow trees, they climbed up the branches and curled up to rest in the crooks of the tree limbs. Each kitten rolled up into a snug ball and went to sleep. The wind and water splashed mud over each kitten. When the rain stopped, the sun dried the mud, and the little gray kittens pushed through the dried mud. Pussy willows, with their tight brown buds from which soft gray tips emerge, grow in memory of the flood and how the willow trees saved the kittens.

Once upon a time, a beautiful princess and a handsome prince were in love, but enemies of the prince captured him, and the princess asked what she could do to gain him his freedom. The prince's captors said the princess had thirty days to spin ten thousand skeins of linen thread, or else they would kill the prince. This seemed like an impossible task, but the princess asked her three cats to help her. With the cats and the princess working day and night, they finished the job, and the prince was freed. Ever since, cats have had the ability to purr, making a sound like the whirring of a spinning wheel.

Some legends explain how cats were created. One Persian legend says that the cat was created when a magician took a handful of smoke and two bright stars, combined them, and produced a gray kitten with shining eyes. Another story says that when the animals were all aboard the ark, Noah was afraid that the lions might attack and eat him and his family.

He asked God for help, and God gave the lions each a bad cold, making them too miserable to hunt. That solved that problem, but then Noah began to worry that the mice would eat all of the stored food. Once again, he asked God for help, and, in answer, one of the lions sneezed and created the cat.

Of course, this contradicts another legend that says that when Noah was loading all of the animals two by two, the cats were the last to board. As they sauntered slowly into the ark, Noah lost patience and slammed the door on their tails, and that's why Turkish Van cats have red tails.

Another story explains why the Manx cat is tailless. It all started when the Vikings invaded the Isle of Man and decided that they wanted the long, beautiful tails of the local cats as decorations for their helmets. The mother cats chewed off their kittens' tails at birth so the Vikings couldn't catch the kittens later for their tails.

Cats have frequently been associated with gods and goddesses, and, sometimes, the cats themselves have been elevated to these positions. Norse legend has Freya's chariot drawn by two large cats, and Dawon is a ferocious tiger ridden into battle by the goddess Durga. In China, farmers worshiped cat goddess Li Shou for her help with fertility and pest control. And no mention of the worship of cats would be complete without Egypt. All cats were worshipped and protected in Egypt, and thousands were mummified after their deaths, but there was also the cat goddess Bastet, guardian of the pharaoh and defender of Ra, the sun good.

The maneki neko, or "beckoning cat," of Japan represents the goddess of mercy. The story goes that a cat sitting outside a temple raised her paw to the emperor (some versions say it was a wealthy merchant) as he was passing. Charmed by the gesture, the emperor turned and entered the temple. Moments after entering the temple, lightning struck the spot where the emperor had been standing. The cat had saved his life.

You can buy maneki neko for good luck in your own home. They come in assorted colors and are made of various materials. The cat is typically represented as a bobtail cat with one paw raised to the head. If the left paw is raised, it's supposed to attract customers into a business. If the right paw is raised, it beckons good fortune and money. If both paws are raised, the cat offers protection. A quick look at these cats on *Amazon.com* indicates that even their colors have meaning. Gold or yellow signifies wealth, of course, but there's also white for good health, black to ward off bad spirits, red for a successful career, pink for love, purple for friendship, and green for academic achievement. Some sources say that calico, the traditional color combination, is the luckiest, which makes sense because

the real Japanese Bobtail, when calico, is considered lucky.

Amazon.com offers another twist to the legend, saying that the most popular version of the legend involves a stray cat and an impoverished shop owner. The owner took in the cat, and the cat would then sit outside the shop. "The cute cat, sitting on hind legs with one paw beckoning, eventually turned around the shop owner's misfortunes." Even if they never bring you wealth or good fortune, maneki neko are pretty cute decorations for cat lovers.

71 Cat Superstitions

Cats have been the subject of superstitions and folk sayings for years, with the cat sometimes bringing good luck and sometimes bad. According to Norse legend, all cats were sacred to Freya, and farmers would leave out bowls of milk for cats to ensure that Freya blessed them with bountiful harvests. When a bride had good weather for her wedding, it was said that she had "fed the cat well." Further, if any cat appeared at a wedding, it was a sign that the marriage would be happy.

The Korat, a breed native to Thailand, is believed to bring good luck. According to The International Cat Association (TICA) breed standard, they are the color of silver, so they signify wealth. They are the color of rain clouds, with eyes the color of young plants, representing good harvests. Because they have heart-shaped faces, a pair of Korat given to a bride ensures a strong and fortunate marriage.

Dating back to the 1700s, there is a belief that if a cat washes behind her ear, a stranger will appear. By the 1920s, this had been refined to the belief that if the cat washed behind the right ear, the stranger would be a man, or if behind the left ear, a woman.

The superstition in the United States says that black cats are unlucky. If one crosses your path, for instance, you'll have bad luck. In Asia and the United Kingdom, it's the opposite; in fact, a black cat is a lucky wedding gift. In Japan, black cats are good luck charms, and even a dream of a black cat is thought to be lucky. In Scotland, a strange black cat on your porch means prosperity. In ancient Egypt, black cats were considered sacred. If you find a white hair on a black cat, that's also good luck, but don't pluck that hair, or your luck will turn bad.

Apparently, if a black cat crosses your path while you're driving, you should turn your hat backward and mark an X on your windshield to avert bad luck. It seems to me you'd be inviting an accident with all of that fumbling around, and what if you weren't wearing a hat? Or, if you were already wearing a baseball cap backward, would turning it the right way around do the trick?

The silver-coated Korat, with its green eyes, is thought to signify good luck.

Superstitions surrounding black cats vary from country to country.

Assigning good or bad luck to a black cat can be harmless fun, but it wasn't always so harmless. Pilgrims in Plymouth distrusted and feared anything they associated with witches, and that included black cats. No black cat was safe at any time of year, but the start of Lent was a particularly bad time, with black cats being burned on Shrove Tuesday to protect homes from fire in the coming year.

For many years, people believed that if you saw a cat with his tail toward a fire, you could expect bad luck. Additional folklore says that you will always be lucky if you know how to make friends with strange cats, that killing a cat will bring you seventeen years bad luck, and that if you take even one of a cat's nine lives, it will haunt you forever.

According to *Ghost Cats* author Dusty Rainbolt, the folks at London's Savoy Grill consider cats good luck. The superstition is that the first person rising from a dinner table of thirteen will meet a terrible end. In 1898, such a party met at the Savoy, and Woolf Joel was the first to leave the table. Shortly after, he was shot dead. Since then, the Savoy always provides a fourteenth guest to any parties of thirteen: a three-foot-high wooden sculpture of a black cat named Kasper. They originally would add a staff member to the table, but then they commissioned artist Basil Ionides to create Kasper in the 1920s.

A myth that has been around since the 1600s—and still persists in spite of being totally false—is that cats can, and do, suck the breath from babies. The reasons range from the cat being drawn to the smell of milk on the baby's breath to the cat being jealous of the baby when the cat is no longer the center of attention. In 2000, a woman claimed that her cat had killed her child. In reality, the child had died from Sudden Infant Death Syndrome. Unfortunately, sometimes infants die unexpectedly. Blaming the cat may be a way of making some sense out of the death, but, in the end, it's totally untrue that cats suck the breath out of babies.

PART XII

Organizations for Cat People

There are more than forty cat registries scattered all over the world. Some are regional, some are national or international, and some are federations of registries, created to help standardize breed descriptions as well as how particular breeds are to be judged.

The Fédération Internationale Féline (FiFe) boasts a forty-country membership that includes all of Europe as well as Argentina, Brazil, Colombia, Mexico, Israel, Indonesia, and Malaysia. Member organizations agree to follow the same rules "with regard to the breed standards, breeding and registration, cattery names, shows, judges and student judges." It is the only organization that counts both the Don Sphynx and the Peterbald in its list of recognized breeds, which seems strange because, according to most sources, the original name of the breed was Don Sphnyx, but it was changed to Peterbald. No matter what you call it, it's the same cat.

The World Cat Federation (WCF) is based in Germany and has 370 member organizations. It generally promotes international contacts between member clubs. Breeders who are members of affiliated clubs may register their cattery names internationally. The WCF participates in the consultations of the European parliament and is jointly responsible for the development of animal-protection laws. They recognize 102 breeds. The Brazilian Shorthair International Cat Society is the only American club that is a member of WCF.

Peterbald

Young Brazilian Shorthair

The World Cat Congress (WCC) is an international federation of the largest organizations and national associations, founded in 1996 "to promote better understanding and cooperation among the world's major cat associations in matters of mutual interest and concern such as cat legislation and feline welfare which affects all cat lovers, from the pedigree breeder to the pet owner." Areas of cooperation include registration, cat-related legislation, feline health, educational material, recognition of pedigrees, and show dates.

There are nine members of the WCC. They are the Australian Cat Federation (ACF); Cat Fanciers Association (CFA); Co-ordinating Cat Council of Australia (CCC of A); FiFe; Governing Council of the Cat Fancy, United Kingdom (GCCF); New Zealand Cat Fancy (NZCF); Southern Africa Cat Council (SACC); The International Cat Association (TICA), and WCF.

In addition to the main cat organizations in the United States—CFA, TICA, and the American Cat Fanciers Association (ACFA)—there are several smaller American cat registries: the American Association of Cat Enthusiasts (AACE), the American Cat Association (ACA) , the Cat Fanciers Federation (CFF), and the United Feline Organization. TICA is based in the United States but has affiliated societies around the world.

If you live near the Canadian border, you can access the Canadian Cat Association (*www.cca-afc.com*) for information on their recognized breeds and cat shows. The CCA was started in 1960 "to promote the welfare of all the cats in Canada, to further the improvement of all breeds of cats in Canada, and to maintain a registry of purebred cats."

Before 1960, all pedigreed cats in Canada had to be registered in the United States or Europe, and all cat shows in Canada were held under the rules of United States associations. Today, the CCA has more than 190,000 registered cats with affiliated clubs across the country.

Bengal

Ragdoll

Just as cats are not small dogs, a cat show is not the same as a dog show. The only thing that dog shows and cat shows have in common is that each animal is judged as to how closely it meets the ideal of the breed standard, and there are championship points awarded. That's where the similarity ends. Even cat shows differ in certain ways, such as rules, point schedules, and titles, which will vary depending on the association presenting the show.

Generally, there are at least six rings. Each ring has cages on three sides, with a judge's table in the center, and the fourth side open to the public. Cats are placed in the cages from the back, and the judge removes each cat from the front, one at a time, placing each cat on the judge's table and evaluating him or her according to the breed standard. The table is sanitized between cats, and each cage is cleaned before the next cat is put in.

Unlike dog shows, where classes are divided by sex, the sexes are judged together at cat shows. There are classes for kittens (between four and eight months old), a champion class for intact cats, and a premier class for altered (neutered/spayed) cats. Household pets are in the HHP class. Household pets are judged on health, appearance, and personality. Occasionally, there may be a veterans class for cats seven years or older.

Each ring is its own show, and each cat shows in each ring. At the end of the day, each judge selects his or her top cats, including Best in Show, with a ring clerk recording the points. A cat who goes Best in Show in Ring 1 might place third in Ring 2

A judge evaluates an entry in comparison to its breed standard.

and not at all in Ring 3. Some shows may, at the end of a weekend, award a Best of the Best from all of the Bests in Show, but that's not common with CFA or TICA. The AFCA awards the top three Bests in Show over a weekend, and the CCA awards the top three Bests in Show on Saturday and then on Sunday, followed by a Best of the Best for the highest overall score of the weekend.

If the cat-show process seems confusing to read about, it's because it's probably easier to do it than to read about it. Once you've gone to a show or two, you'll soon understand all of the ins and outs. If you know someone who shows his or her cat, go to some shows with that person just to watch so that you'll have a general understanding when you decide to enter your own cat. But remember: no matter what happens at a show, the best cat is the one curled up on your own lap.

CFA SHOWS:
A BRIEF SUMMARY

At CFA shows, household pets receive ribbons of merit. All other cats compete for points to become either a Champion or Grand Champion (intact cats) or a Premier or Grand Premier (altered cats). Cats who win six winners ribbons become a Champion or a Premier. A Champion who then wins two hundred points is a Grand Champion. A Premier needs seventy-five points to become a Grand Premier.

The best cat wins one point for each cat defeated. The second best gets 95 percent of the points awarded to the best cat. The third best gets 90 percent of the points; the fourth best, 85 percent; and so on down the line to tenth place. At the end of the show season, which runs from May 1 to April 30, a cat is credited with the points from his or her highest one hundred rings. A kitten is credited with his or her highest forty rings.

TICA TITLES

TICA offers Champion, Champion Alter, and, for household pets, Master titles. For each of these, a cat must earn three hundred points plus one final award. TICA doesn't award Best of Breed ribbons. Points are given to the top five placing cats: first place gets twenty-five points; second place, twenty points; third, fifteen points; fourth, ten points; and fifth, five points. That's fairly straightforward, except that a judge will give out five Best of Color Awards to, say, five of the best black Persians, and then he or she will choose the top five from the division (i.e., the top five solid-colored Persians), which may or may not include one of those black Persians. Then the judge will award first-, second-, and third-place Best of Breed placements that include all of the Persian colors.

Going up the ladder, TICA titles include:

- Champion/Master
- Grand Champion/Grand Master
- Double Grand Champion/Double Grand Master
- Triple Grand Champion/Triple Grand Master
- Quadruple Grand Champion/Quadruple Grand Master
- Supreme Grand Champion/Supreme Grand Master

The American Cat Fanciers Association (AFCA) was founded in 1955 and, according to the group's website, is known as the "fairest, friendliest, and most fun feline association." The ACFA works to promote the welfare of all domesticated purebred and nonpurebred cats as well as to increase education and knowledge of those cats.

The ACFA offers a Junior ACFA Program for those between the ages of seven and seventeen. This program focuses on exhibiting and education, with knowledgeable adults offering age-appropriate classes on such topics as grooming, handling, behaviors, basic feline first aid, and show clerking and stewarding techniques.

The ACFA recognizes fifty-four breeds: Abyssinian, American Bobtail, American Curl, American Shorthair, American Wirehair, Australian Mist, Balinese, Bengal, Birman, Bombay, British Longhair, British Shorthair, Burmese, Burmilla, Chartreux, Cornish Rex, Cymric, Devon Rex, Egyptian Mau, European Burmese, Exotic Shorthair, Havana Brown, Himalayan, Japanese Bobtail, Korat, Kurilian Bobtail, Longhair Exotic, LaPerm, Maine Coon Cat, Manx, Nebelung, Norwegian Forest Cat, Ocicat, Oriental Longhair, Oriental Shorthair, Persian, Peterbald, Pixiebob, RagaMuffin, Ragdoll, Russian Blue, Russian Shorthair, Scottish Fold Longhair, Scottish Fold Shorthair, Selkirk Rex, Siamese, Siberian, Singapura, Snowshoe, Somali, Sphynx, Tonkinese, Turkish Angora, Turkish Van.

Siberian

Abyssinian

The Cat Fanciers' Association (CFA) was founded in 1906 after some of its members broke ties with the American Cat Association. Its objectives are "the welfare of all cats; the promotion and improvement of CFA recognized breeds of cats; the registering, recording, or identifying by number or by other means the names and/or pedigrees of cats and kittens; the promulgation of rules for the management of cat shows; the licensing of cat shows held under the rules of this organization; and the promotion of the interests of breeders and exhibitors of pedigreed cats."

The CFA licenses about four hundred shows each season and has more than six hundred member clubs. Besides licensing conformation cat shows, they also offer agility at some shows. There's a CFA Ambassador Program that helps educate fanciers and explain how cat shows work. Participants wear buttons at events that say, "Ask Me."

CFA also offers two mentoring programs. One is for adults, in which fanciers are paired with mentors to learn about showing and/or breeding. The other is the Youth Feline Education Program for those between the ages of seven and eighteen. Opportunities include doing breed presentations, working on show committees, or working with therapy cats. The program gives students a chance to learn more about cats at their own pace.

The CFA recognizes forty-two pedigreed breeds: Abyssinian, American Bobtail, American Curl, American Shorthair, American Wirehair, Balinese, Bengal, Birman, Bombay, British Shorthair, Burmese, Burmilla, Chartreux, Colorpoint Shorthair, Cornish Rex, Devon Rex, Egyptian Mau, European Burmese, Exotic, Havana Brown, Japanese Bobtail, Korat, LaPerm, Maine Coon, Manx, Norwegian Forest Cat, Ocicat, Oriental, Persian, Ragamuffin, Ragdoll, Russian Blue, Scottish Fold, Selkirk Rex, Siamese, Siberian, Singapura, Somali, Sphynx, Tonkinese, Turkish Angora, and Turkish Van. (A note regarding the Scottish Fold: Currently only folded-ear cats of Scottish lineage are allowed in the show ring.)

Burmese

LaPerm

The International Cat Association (TICA) is the world's largest registry of pedigreed and household pet cats and was the first to allow household cats to compete in shows on equal footing with pedigreed cats. TICA's mission is to promote the health and welfare of all domestic cats by educating breeders, owners, exhibitors, and the general public; to offer a comprehensive pedigree registry; to hold sanctioned cat shows; to encourage TICA members to take active roles in the community, such as through work at local animal shelters and outreach programs for schools; and to promote responsible cat-related legislation.

TICA's Junior Exhibitors Program for anyone under the age of eighteen is a program of six levels, with each level having different activities and tests. Students learn about TICA, the procedures of showing, and cat health and welfare. At the senior levels, there's emphasis on cat breeds and working at shows. The TICA Therapy Pet Program offers titles as a way to recognize people who have therapy cats.

TICA administers the rules for the licensing and management of cat shows in 104 countries and also sponsors International Cat Agility Tournaments (ICAT). The organization recognizes seventy-one breeds of cats, and some of these are the longhaired or shorthaired varieties of a particular breed. In this list, SH equals Shorthair and LH equals Longhair.

TICA breeds are Abyssinian, American Bobtail, American Bobtail LH, American Curl, American Curl LH, American Shorthair, American Wirehair, Australian Mist, Balinese, Bengal, Bengal LH, Birman, Bombay, British Longhair, British Shorthair, Burmese, Burmilla, Burmilla LH, Chartreux, Chausie, Cornish Rex, Cymric, Devon Rex, Donskoy, Egyptian Mau, Exotic Shorthair, Havana, Himalayan, Japanese Bobtail, Japanese Bobtail LH, Khaomanee, Korat, Kurilian Bobtail, Kurilian Bobtail LH, LaPerm, LaPerm SH, Lykoi, Maine Coon, Maine Coon Polydactyl, Manx, Minuet, Minuet Longhair, Munchkin, Munchkin LH, Nebulung, Norwegian Forest, Ocicat, Oriental Longhair, Oriental Shorthair, Persian, Peterbald, Pixiebob, Pixiebob Longhair, Ragdoll, Russian Blue, Savannah, Scottish Fold, Scottish LH, Scottish Straight, Scottish Straight LH, Selkirk Rex, Selkirk Rex LH, Siamese, Siberian, Singapura, Snowshoe, Somali, Sphynx, Thai, Tonkinese, Toyger, Turkish Angora, and Turkish Van.

Breeds that are not yet fully recognized, that may show, but not win points, are the Highlander, Highlander SH, Minskin, and Serengeti.

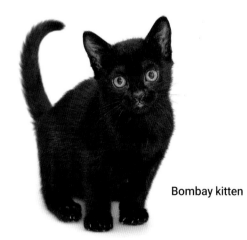

Bombay kitten

Registries and Cat Shows

AMERICAN CAT FANCIERS ASSOCIATION (ACFA)
www.acfacat.com

CAT FANCIERS ASSOCIATION (CFA)
www.cfa.org

THE INTERNATIONAL CAT ASSOCIATION (TICA)
www.tica.org

Adoption Sites

ADOPT A PET
www.adoptapet.com

PETFINDER
www.petfinder.com

PETSMART CHARITIES
www.petsmartcharities.org (many Petsmart stores have adoption days in coordination with local shelters)

Medical and Health-Related Sites

NOTE: These sites are for reference only, to help you understand a particular disease or find a practitioner. *Do not rely on the Internet to diagnose and treat ailments in your cat. Too many diseases and illnesses have similar symptoms and, even if you get it right, a treatment that works for one cat may not be appropriate for yours. Your own veterinarian is your best resource for keeping your cat healthy.*

AMERICAN VETERINARY CHIROPRACTIC ASSOCIATION
www.animalchiropractic.org

AMERICAN VETERINARY MEDICAL ASSOCIATION
www.avma.org

ASPCA ANIMAL POISON CONTROL CENTER
888-426-4435 (consultation fee charged)

CATHEALTH
www.cathealth.com

CORNELL UNIVERSITY'S FELINE HEALTH CENTER
www.vet.cornell.edu/fhc

INTERNATIONAL VETERINARY ACUPUNCTURE SOCIETY
www.ivas.org

PETMD
www.petmd.com

PET POISON HELPLINE
855-764-7661 (consultation fee charged)

VCA VETERINARY HOSPITALS
www.vcahospitals.com

VETINFO
www.vetinfo.com

VET ORGANICS
www.vet-organics.com

VETSTREET
www.vetstreet.com

WEBMD PETS
pets.webmd.com

Pet Sitters

NATIONAL ASSOCIATION OF PROFESSIONAL PET SITTERS
www.petsitters.org

PET SITTERS ASSOCIATES, LLC
www.petsitllc.com

PET SITTERS INTERNATIONAL
www.petsit.com

ROVER
www.rover.com

Cat Agility

CAT FANCIERS' ASSOCIATION AGILITY
agility.cfa.org/index.shtml

INTERNATIONAL CAT AGILITY TOURNAMENTS (ICAT)
www.catagility.com

Therapy Work

PET PARTNERS
www.petpartners.org

General and Fun Information

THE MESSY BEAST
www.messybeast.com

Index

Acknowledgments

Thank you to William Seleen, DVM, who gave me his email address and always responded quickly to my questions. Thank you to Bev Caldwell and Dusty Rainbolt for their encouragement, suggestions, and support. Thank you to the members of the Cat Writers' Association, who shared thoughts and opinions on a myriad of topics, but especially to Marva Marrow and Lynn Miller; Teresa Keigher, CFA judge; Vickie Fisher, TICA judge; and Betty Sleep of Carraig Birmans, who tried to explain showing to me. Thanks to Julie Janson, I *think* I got it right. Thanks also to Anthony Nichols, who explained showing in Great Britain.

Photo Credits

Key: r (right), l (left), t (top), b (bottom)

Shutterstock: 10 FACE (151); 135pixels (107); absolutimages (76, 123, 149 b, 179); Africa Studio (13, 44 cat, 56, 59, 63, 73, 106 r, 111, 161, 171 l, 171 r, 178, 184, 194 r); Agata Kowalczyk (159); ajlatan (70); Alena Ozerova (49 t, 62); Alexandr Junek Imaging (190); ANCH (38 l); Andrey Kuzmichev (217); Andrey_Kuzmin (68, 72); Andrii_K (200 tr); Anton Gvozdikov (213); ANURAK PONGPATIMET (97, 219); Astrid Gast (122); Axel Bueckert (144); Bachkova Natalia (163); Benjamin Simeneta (158 r); BigNazik (170); Bildagentur Zoonar GmbH (80); Bill Anastasiou (183); bmf-foto.de (120 r); Bornfree (197); Boyloso (32 r); Brenda Carson (204 l); Brooke Becker (164); Bruno Passigatti (173 t); Bulltus_casso (158 l); Bussakorn Ewesakul (175); buteo (188 t); catinsyrup (74); catwalker (196 Garfield stamp, 196 tr); Chendongshan (52, 138); COBRASoft (71); correct pictures (82); Cosmin Manci (118 t); cottonstudio (32 l); Countess-Flora (15 l); Cressida studio (22 t); cworthy (152); Danny Smythe (207); Daria Chichkareva (204 r); de2marco (205 r); De Jongh Photography (78, 131); DenisNata (154); dezy (114); dien (18 r, 36 t, 149 t); Dmitri Ma (89 r, 162); Dmitrij Skorobogatov (54); Dora Zett (18 l); Dorottya Mathe (69 b); Dulce Rubia (79); EcoPrint (11 b, 187 t); effective stock photos (201 r); Elena Butinova (218 l); Elena Rozhenok (156); Elya Vatel (61 l); Eric Isselee (4, 14, 26 r, 27 l, 27 r, 29 l, 33 l, 35, 96, 102, 116, 148, 153, 166, 210, 211 l, 211 r); Erik Lam (29 r); Ermolaev Alexander (106 l, 212 l); Erwin Niemand (187 b); Esin Deniz (127); Evdoha_spb (39); Evgenyi (57, 112); f11photo (193); FCG (19); Fernanda Leite (196 cat); Fesus Robert (200 br); fleabag (95); Foonia (47); Francesco Scotto di Vetta (105); geraldb (200 l); Giedriius (209 t); Gino Santa Maria (115); Gladkova Svetlana (31); goodluz (7); gpeet (223); Grigorita Ko (9, 186); Gutzemberg (front cover); Imageman (75); Irina oxilixo Danilova (199 r); Iryna Imago (132 l); Ivonne Wierink (87 r); Jacques Julien (36 b, 208); Jagodka (216 l); James Steidl (160); Janis Smits (80); Jaromir Chalabala (45); j.chizhe (169); JeepFoto (136); JE Jevgenija (34); Jiranuch Suwanarat (87 l); Jiri Foltyn (110); Joy Baldassarre (203); Jumnong (206); Kachalkina Veronika (101 l); Kadek Jensen (185); Kasefoto (1, 5, 215 r); Kateryna Kon (128); Katho Menden (167); Katrina Elena (58 cat); Koliadzynska Iryna (113); Konstantin Aksenov (46); Kucher Serhii (15 r, 23, 24, 28 b, 30 l, 33 r, 66); Lapina (180); Lara Makela (205 l); Linn Currie (37, 202, 216 r); lkoimages (12); Lux Blue (191); madeinitaly4k (21); Maria Sbytova (137); Martina_L (83); Maslouskaya Alena (28 t); Massimo Cattaneo (99, 134); maxsattana (104 cat); Michael Pettigrew (181); Milles Studio (88); Mr. Master (background numbers on part pages, part numbers); M. Sam (121); mydegage (150); n7atal7i (back cover kitten, 3); Nadinelle (65); Nalaphotos (135); Nana Trongratanawong (201 l); Nataliia Dvukhimenna (117); Nataliya Kuznetsova (25 r); nelik (25 l, 212 r); Nneirda (142); Oksana Kuzmina (48); Okssi (40, 42, 92, 119); Oleksandr Lytvynenko (209 b, 218 r); Oleksandr Rybitskiy (168 r); Ondrej Prosicky (189); Onur ERSIN (77); OoddySmile Studio (89 l); Patrik Slezak (67); Pavel Shlykov (108); Pavel Vinnik (93); Pelagey (157); Peter Radacsi (11 t); Peter Wollinga (6 cat); Phant (94); pio3 (222); Richard Peterson (221); rook76 (195); rossella (109); Ruslan Semichev (91); Samrith Na Lumpoon (173 b); Santi Nanta (98 t); Scampi (38 r); schankz (155); Sebastian Studio (172); Seregraff (192, 220); Serghei Starus (43); Sophie McAulay (60 t); SpeedKingz (139, 140); Stefano Garau (129); Stokkete (176); Susan Schmitz (51, 61 r); Syda Productions (101 r); Szymon Kaczmarczyk (98 b); takakophoto (168 l); Tami Freed (53); tankist276 (22 b); Tanya Sid (86); tatianaput (126); The Len (69 t); thodonal88 (132 r, 145); Tiplyashina Evgeniya (8); Tomas K (49 b); Tompet (81); Tony Campbell (165); Trevor Allen Weddings (55); Tuzemka (60 b); Tyler Olson (141); Ulza (146); Utekhina Anna (16 r); uzhursky (133, 177, 215 l); Valeri Potapova (143); Valerio Pardi (64); Vasiliy Koval (16 l, 30 r, 194 l); vdovin_vn (198); Veera (17); v.gi (120 l); Vitaliy Krasovskiy (199 l); Vladimir Wrangel (188 b); Vladyslav Starozhylov (26 l); Volodymyr Burdiak (10); VP Photo Studio (50); vubaz (118 b); Vydrin (100); WaitForLight (85); wavebreakmedia (125, 147); xu lin feng (182); You Touch Pix of EuToch (103); Zanna Pesnina (130); zlikovec (174); Zotova M (41)

Back cover: freepik.com (award ribbon); **Page 3:** pngtree.com (yarn); **Page 20:** Sunny Schultz by Joanne Leah

About the Author

Susan M. Ewing lives in Jamestown, New York, with her husband, Jim, and writes a bi-weekly column, "The Pet Pen," for *The Post-Journal* of Jamestown, New York. She has written for *Kittens USA, Cats USA,* and *Cats Magazine.* She is the past president of the Cat Writers' Association and her cat flash cards, *Cats! Train Your Owner!* won a Muse medallion and the President's Award from CWA. She was also awarded the Michael S. Brim Distinguished Service Award by the Cat Writers' Association.